Pathways to Success

BY
KEN BENSON
&
AL GRUBE

Edited by Bob Esler

Page design by Bob Esler
Cover design by Bob Esler

ISBN 1-4382-0197-4
EAN 9 781438 201979

Printed in the United States of America
by CreateSpace.com, a division of Amazon.com

This book is available on Amazon.com

Pathways to Success

CONTENTS

We dedicate our book to Bob Esler, our editor and friend. Without Bob's guidance, wisdom, professional savvy and unstinting attention to detail, this book could never have been published.

Prologue

"No Masks"

The masks of tragedy and comedy are the symbols of the theater. Successful theater, be it comedy or tragedy, must convey an illusion of the "first time" to its audience. We have enjoyed theater as an avocation. In many respects, acting may have helped us succeed in the business world. But we both recognize that whatever our successes, they have not been reached by illusion or camouflage. NO MASKS! Candor, truth, trust, honesty, fairness and commitment have been our business practices.

Book One is an assortment of autobiographical sketches that set the stage for Book Two, which describes the fundamentals that we believe are the requirements for PATHWAYS TO SUCCESS.

Book Two illustrates ten principals for the successful management of a business. We have spent the past three years co-authoring our book. We sincerely believe these ten short chapters cover the basic elements for operating a successful business.

Although we are both natives of Wisconsin, are University of Wisconsin graduates and have spent most of our adult lives in Sheboygan County, our business careers, childhood experiences and vision of what we are about are totally different.

That's why we begin in Book One by describing these differences with brief autobiographical sketches. Why bother reading all of this before reading about our business principles in Book Two? We believe that by getting acquainted with each of us you may be able to better understand the ten principles with which we agree. We think our separate, diverse, living and business experiences helped us discover what works and what fails. The differences in our individual careers may broaden the scope of what might work, and not work, for you.

Of course, it is not mandatory that you read Book One before absorbing Book Two. It's up to you. Perhaps you may prefer reading our book backwards; there are no surprise endings!

The ten chapters of Book Two are both a primer about the art of business and an advanced text on how to effectively get things done by working with and leading others. Here we explain how to bring out the best in people by utilizing their strengths and overcoming their weaknesses

Aphorisms are important. Have a vision of your business. Develop a mission statement. Tell the truth. Trust one another. Be fair to your employees. Be fair to your employer. Listen to your employees. Listen to your boss. Listen to your customer. Listen to your stockholders. Listen! Respond! Understand! Communicate in the same language. Be candid!

But the business world is filled with clichés, buzz words, and mindless formulae appearing on the dust covers of thousands of "how to" books. As Macbeth said, "it's a tale told by an idiot, full of sound and fury, signifying nothing."

We could now move forward and puff up our successes, giving you the impression that we know more than we really do. But who are we to do that? We have had both successes and failures. We have each had a lifetime of business experiences that we can account for, but only that. We cannot pretend to offer you a book that will change your lives or make you multi-millionaires. But it may help. Why write a book if everything is so simple? Read on and find out.

Al Grube & Ken Benson
Co-authors

Book One: Two Different Paths

Childhood
College
Military Service
Family
Work
Community

Getting To Know Us

In Book One, Two Different Paths, we include stories from our past that might help explain how we became who we are. As we wrote each story, it stimulated memories of other things that happened to us.

Taken together, these stories give insight into things that influenced us. With this background, one could more easily understand where we were coming from and possibly appreciate why we believe in the principles discussed in Book Two.

We also enjoyed sharing these stories with each other during the writing process. It seemed a shame not to share them with others, so share them we have.

We decided to organize the stories into six categories:

Growing Up

College

Military Service

Family

Work

Community

Ken and Sally Benson, Mary and Al Grube, taken on Al's 79th birthday, July 2, 2007.

Ken Benson's Childhood

Growing up on the farm

I am not a city boy. I was born on August 2, 1929, in the hospital in Mauston, Wisconsin. About one week after my birth, mom and I were back home on the farm. Our farm was located in Juneau County, about three miles west of New Lisbon. We owned 160 acres of land with about 120 acres under plow; the rest was woods and swamp. We were a family of five: mom, dad, my sister Mildred and me plus our hired man, Axel Jensen.

Axel was from North Dakota. He started working for us in 1930 at the age of seventeen and stayed with us for seventeen years. He was a quiet, hardworking, gentle soul who was very talented mechanically, but less effective with animals than my dad.

Growing up on a farm among the sandstone bluffs of rural central Wisconsin was a rare privilege. It was years before I realized how beneficial it was to have enjoyed the quietness and privacy of farm life along with the hard work. There was something different to do in each season, repeated each year as though it was a first time experience.

Sometimes the awesome beauty of the countryside overwhelmed the monotony of cross-cultivating those rows of checked corn with a one-horse cultivator. But monotony provides a space for exciting thoughts and dreams about the future rather than boredom.

The farm near New Lisbon, where Ken spent his childhood, after a Spring snowfall on April 15, 1947

Illness

Until about my first birthday, I was a normal, healthy baby boy. But then I started losing weight and became seriously ill. Dr. Hess frequently visited our home, but didn't seem to know how to deal with my undiagnosed malady. My condition continued to deteriorate. Mom and dad finally changed doctors. They called Dr. Stames from New Lisbon to come to my aid. I started showing some signs of improvement in December of 1930 and was finally on the road to recovery. Needless to say, Dr. Stames became our family doctor and was credited with my cure.

It was not until I received my college physical at the University of Wisconsin in 1947 that a doctor's post diagnosis of my infant illness was identified as rheumatic fever. The University doctor based his retroactive diagnosis upon the fact that my heart had a murmur, beat occasionally in couplets, and was enlarged.

Dad worked as a dance hall inspector at the nearby Twin Bluffs Dance Hall for $5 a night to help pay off my medical expenses. The farm was heavily mortgaged and dad was unable to make ends meet during those depression years. To make matters worse, he lost his dairy herd to Bangs disease. Dad had to ship out the cattle and start over again, but only after he fumigated the barn and was certified by the state that it was safe to acquire cattle once again.

Life on the Farm

Farm life is both healthy and lonely. I had few playmates; there were no children my age in our immediate neighborhood. I did have my sister Mildred who is four years older than me. Mil was quite protective and we enjoyed being together most of the time. I think I probably was more responsible for the few times we fought.

In summer, I did have a friend nearby. Dick Leicht spent summers with his uncle, Dr. Stetler, a New Lisbon dentist, and his wife. They spent summers in a little cottage nestled at the base of one of the twin

The Benson family in the early 1940s: Ken, Mom, Dad and Mil

bluffs about one mile north of our farm. I would often hike over to the Stetler cottage and play games with Dick; he would also occasionally visit our farm.

The Twin Bluff Dance Hall was located directly across the road from Dr. Stetler's cottage. The front entrance of the dance hall led into the bar which stretched across the entire front of the building. A large dance hall extended behind the bar to the very rear of the building. There was a handrail around the periphery of the dance hall separating the dancers from the sitters and talkers. This is the same dance hall where my dad worked as a bouncer when I was ill as an infant with rheumatic fever. At least once each week, dance bands filled the smoke-filled hall with the music of polkas, waltzes and other dance music.

Dick and I walked over to the dance hall one hot summer afternoon in July to offer our services for hire to the owners, the Petersons. They asked if we would pick off all the gum that had accumulated under the handrails; we agreed to do this if we each were paid ten cents. They accepted our proposal and we spent the rest of the afternoon chipping off wads of gum from underneath the rail. We were amazed at the number of gum chewing dancers that had made their deposit under the rail before they entered the dance floor for a romantic interlude.

Mom always had a strawberry bed in her garden. One day Dick and I picked thirteen quarts of berries; mom was pleased with our endeavor. Later in the day, she asked me where the berries were. I explained that Dick and I had delivered them to the Petersons at the Twin Bluff Dance Hall; we had sold them for thirteen cents a quart. She was upset. We had picked the patch clean for the day; there were no strawberries on our kitchen table that evening for supper.

Gordon Barnes lived on a large farm located a few miles northwest of our farm. We always spent the Fourth of July together shooting off fireworks. We would

A 10-year-old Ken leads a calf outside the barn on his family farm. In preparation for showing the calf at 4-H competitions, Ken had to train it to lead.

save our money many weeks prior to the big day and buy every kind of fireworks our total savings of about sixty-five cents permitted. We blew up cans, ignited firecrackers, cherry bombs, pinwheels and sparklers until everything went up in flames and our money was spent. We would each buy a pint of Rothe's ice cream as the final special treat on this very special day.

Gordon and I worked on 4-H projects together. He would show Guernseys and I would show Holsteins at the Juneau County Fair in Mauston. We were both excellent showmen and received blue ribbons in showmanship. We also won many blue ribbons on our calves. We slept on the hay and straw piled in the empty stable adjacent to our animals. We took every ride on the fairgrounds, ate everything offered at the food stands and looked in awe at the exciting life of the hucksters traveling the fair circuit.

Work was our life

Dairy farming is a demanding occupation. The day started about 5:30 a.m. and ended about 8:30 p.m. When I was in the fourth grade, I milked four cows by hand each morning and evening. Then, when I was twelve, we bought a two-unit De Laval milking machine. I soon became an expert in machine milking our twenty milk cows. Axel ran one unit and I ran the other. After I became a teenager, I would generally milk the entire herd in less than an hour, running both units myself. By then we had the luxury of having every third Sunday off. What a wonderful perk to have that third Sunday free of chores.

The ritual of farming revolved around the dairy cow. We milked the cows twice a day, seven days a week. We cleaned the barn each day; we fed the cows silage and ground feed before milking and hay afterwards. We climbed into the silo to fork out the corn silage, throwing it down the shoot to the silo room. Twice each day, we threw hay down the hay shoots from

Ken's dad, Carl

the hay mows spreading it in front of the cows after milking. We bedded the cows with straw after cleaning the barn each morning. We limed the center aisle running between the gutters under the manure carrier track. I curried the milk cows daily after walking home from school. We also cared for the heifers in the heifer barn and the calves in the calf pens. We had about fifty animals to provide for.

We planted oats, corn and hay and harvested the crops to feed and bed the cattle. In addition, we had about two hundred Leghorn hens, four sows and twenty-four baby pigs to provide for. Mom would care for the chickens and sell the eggs; her "egg money" was used to buy groceries and other sundries. The little pigs would be fattened and marketed when they passed the two hundred pound mark. They lived under the straw stack on the north end of the barn yard, opposite the hog house. Dad had a large cast iron cooker in the hog house. He would make a mash out of potatoes and skim milk, sometimes using brewery malt as part of the feed supplements. The cooker was also used to boil water when we were butchering a hog for our own food supplies.

Dad used the revenue from shipping pigs to market to pay interest on the mortgage. In the winter when the cattle were all in the barn, we would spend each Saturday morning grinding feed. Our hammermill was in the granary, belt powered by our Allis-Chalmers tractor. We ground oats and corn mixing in high protein linseed oil meal and other supplements as we ground the feed. Chickens mash and hog feed required separate formulae.

After harvest in the fall, we plowed the fields. In the winter, dad and Axel would harvest lumber and firewood from our forty-acre woodland. They would haul the logs on a sled over the snow to a sawmill for lumber and we would saw the limbs into cord wood for our kitchen stove and space heater. We had neither central heating nor a bathroom in our house. We did have cold running water and a reservoir in our wood-burning kitchen stove to heat the water.

With spring came an exciting rebirth after the long, cold, snow-filled winter. As soon as the frost was out of the ground we would start

The Benson farmhouse.

working the land in preparation for planting. By mid-April, dad would start planting oats. Alfalfa or clover seed was planted with the oats so that the biennial hay crop would grow the following year after the annual oats crop was harvested. He would harness a team of three horses for this task. Sometimes he would also plant a small crop of wheat and barley. We had four horses and also had the services of Monarch, a cooperatively-owned stallion we shared with several farmers.

Corn was not planted until May after the last frost. We had to cultivate this crop throughout the summer. I was given the task of cross cultivating the checked corn with a one-horse cultivator. Billy, a large Belgium horse, was my assigned horse for this task. I would clean the horse barn, feed, curry and harness Billy and head out to the long, narrow corn fields to cross-cultivate them until finished. This task would have to be repeated several times during the summer. Day after day, I would proceed shirtless up and down each corn row with Billy pulling the cultivator and the sun on my back. I didn't wear a straw hat and my face and back tended to burn more than tan.

Movies, Motorcycles and Mayhem

I was fourteen years old and had a Wisconsin driver's license permitting me to drive during daylight hours. My mom and dad left the farm for a Sunday visit with friends. I was home alone with the car and had the day off until milking time in the evening.

I drove to New Lisbon and picked up my friend, Tom Mason. We drove to the neighboring town of Mauston to see the matinee. After the movie, Tom asked me if he could drive; I gave him the keys and he slid into the driver's seat. He did not have a driver's license but he knew how to drive. We drove to New Lisbon and then drove around the downtown. As we approached the movie theater, the moviegoers were exiting. Tom's brother Joe was also leaving the theater. Tom stopped the car at the U. S. Highway 12 arterial sign, then slowly crossed the road. Suddenly, mayhem.

A speeding motorcycle loudly clipped the rear right fender of dad's car. The two motorcycle passengers were propelled into the air and slammed into a lamppost on the sidewalk. They were screaming in pain and bloody. Sirens were next as the police arrived.

Tom quickly slid over toward the passenger seat and said, "You get behind the wheel!"

Joe witnessed both the accident and Tom's effort to get me behind the steering wheel.

Joe ran up to the front passenger side car window and shouted at Tom, "You idiot! Get back behind the wheel; there were three hundred witnesses to this accident. They all saw you driving the car. Tom sheepishly slid over to the driver's seat position.

The ambulance transported the two injured motorcyclists to the hospital. The police measured the scene of the accident and interviewed witnesses. They asked Tom for his driver's license; then promptly issued him a ticket for driving a motor vehicle without a license when he failed to produce one. They charged the motorcycle driver with inattentive driving.

That evening as I began milking the cows, my dad returned from a pleasant afternoon with friends. I dreaded the moment, but finally mustered the courage to confess the unpleasant truth of my afternoon at the movies with Tom. Dad was severe; he was especially concerned about the injured. I didn't know the answers. Dad phoned the police and found that the two motorcyclists had sustained only minor injuries. He perceived the pain I was suffering from my breach of trust to him; he was less severe than I had anticipated.

Mil and Ken hold Skippy's puppies. Skippy was Ken's dog which he enjoyed for 14 years of his life.

Several weeks later during the middle of haying season, I was summoned to appear in Juneau County Court in Mauston as a witness in the case. Dad was upset about interrupting the haying on a sunny day, leaving the winnowed hay crop in the field while we drove to court.

I nervously took the witness stand and truthfully testified about the accident, as I recalled it. The charges against Tom were dropped because he was a minor. Tom was relieved as he intently listened to the judge's stern lecture about obeying the law and driving safely when he could legally do so. The motorcycle driver paid a small fine for inattentive driving.

About a week later I was surprised to receive a witness fee check in the mail in the amount of $6.40. Dad had always paid me twenty cents a day during haying season. He didn't make any comments about the disparity in pay scale between witnessing and haying

Threshing

Dad and Mike Verbsky, our neighbor, became partners in the purchase of a McCormick-Deering threshing machine. They agreed to thresh the oats for about eight farmers in our neighborhood at a charge of four cents per bushel. Prior to that, a large steel-wheeled steam engine would come through the neighborhood pulling a huge threshing machine. The machine required more than twenty people to run. With dad and Mike's machine, only twelve people were needed to keep everything moving.

About two weeks before threshing time, dad would harness up three horses, hitch them up to the grain binder and start cutting the grain. The binder left a neat row of bundles of oats; each bundle was automatically tied precisely in the middle with binder twine. Axel, our hired man, and I would shock the grain; dad would also help after he had finished cutting the thirty-acre oat crop. We picked up a bundle of grain in each hand by the top, firmly setting the base of the two bundles on the oats stubble; the oat-laden tops were pitched upward toward each other at an angle that would permit them to be self-standing. We would repeat this process with three sets of bundles side by side creating a tent like shock of grain; then we would put a bundle on the top of the shock as a cap for rain protection.

Haying

When threshing time arrived, all the farmers in the neighborhood helped each other until all the grain at each farm was threshed. It was a joint effort.

Threshing

Mike Verbsky generally watched over the threshing machine to see that all the chains and belts were moving in the right direction and properly lubricated. When the thresher was at our farm, dad would stack the straw that was blown vigorously through the long blower pipe extending from the end of the machine. One man would bag the kernels of oats that gravity flowed down through a pipe into the bags from the dumper located on top of the machine. Two men would haul the threshed grain to the granary and empty the bags into the bins.

Threshing was a social experience. All the farmers' wives helped each other feed the crews. The meals were hearty and special. Beef pot roast, gravy, mashed potatoes, carrots, peas, Jello salad and warm apple pie with ice cream and coffee. At noon, everything shut down and the dirty, sweaty and happy farmers all sat around the table chatting good naturedly and eating heartily. In the evening, supper was served about 5:30 p.m. Wieners or cold cuts were often served as the meat of choice for this meal along with potato salad, cake and ice cream. Roast chicken, fried chicken, roast pork and pork chops were also served at some of the meals.

The last farm to be threshed on the circuit was special, for this was when a keg of beer would be tapped to celebrate the end of the oat harvest. One or two of the farmers would sometimes overindulge. This was the first time I saw someone drunk. Paul Paulson was driving his team home under the influence and I think that might have been true of Gilbert Ormson as well. But no harm was done. I am not sure how everyone managed to get their chores done when they got home.

Porky

Dad was very watchful when a sow was about to give birth to a litter of pigs in the hog house. He scrubbed down the birth pen with disinfectant, placed clean straw from the straw stack on the floor and built a wooden shelter about six inches wide around the perimeter of the pen as a protective area for the baby pigs to hide under as they grew old enough to run about.

One cold, March day a sow gave birth to thirteen baby pigs. She only had twelve nipples to feed her litter. I took on the responsibility for Porky, the nipple-less orphan. I took Porky into the dining room of our house and placed him in a cardboard box behind the wood stove. I held him in my arms and bottle fed him with milk several times each day and night. After each feeding, Porky snuggled in his bedded box behind the friendly, warm wood fire of the stove.

It was only a matter of two weeks before Porky became my very devoted pet. He would follow me all around the farmyard and even wagged his tail. Pigs are very intelligent and also clean animals if provided the opportunity. I treated Porky much the same as a puppy and he loved me; in his eyes, I was his mother. As the weeks passed and the rest of the litter was weaned, we tried to place Porky back in the pen with his siblings. He was summarily rejected by his family and ruthlessly picked on by his brothers and sisters.

Dad took him out of the hog house pen and placed him alone in a specially built pen in the corner of the horse barn. There I fed him and let him loose whenever I was outside. Porky would affectionately nuzzle me, wag his tail and follow me about the yard. I enjoyed his companionship but felt a bit self-conscious when the school bus passed our house and the high school kids in the bus would laugh and point at me followed by a pig.

By the time Porky was six months old, his siblings weighed more than two hundred pounds each and were ready for market. Porky was a little lighter, but about a month after his brothers and sisters had been sent to market, dad sold him to our neighbor, Harold Schubert. I had reluctantly become reconciled with the fact that Porky would be butchered. It wasn't easy for me; I hated to see him hauled away to the Schubert farm. I just had to reckon with the facts of farm life in spite of my pain.

A few days after Porky's departure I was in the woodshed gathering an arm load of wood for the kitchen stove. It was dark outside. As I squatted down to pile the arm load of fire wood on my left arm, I felt something nuzzle my back. I dropped the wood, turned around and there was Porky wagging his curled tail, happily greeting me. I was devastated and happy at the same time. I had missed my pet and he was back in my arms, yet I knew that dad would return him to Harold Schubert, his new owner.

I said good bye a second time to my wonderful pet and sorrowfully saw him returned to the Schubert farm to await his butchering.

The Little Red School

Mom and dad decided that I could begin my first grade education at the age of five in The Little Red School, located about one-half mile north of the farm. I lasted for two weeks! Each day of this new experience I came home sad, looking poorly, my appetite gone. Mom and dad wisely reconsidered and let me stay home for a year before I started the first grade once again, this time with a more mature outlook.

Catherine Niles was the teacher for all eight grades in The Little Red School. Ironically, the building was white. We had electricity, but no running water. We had a vitreous china crock called a bubbler located on a table in the front hall which we filled with drinking water from the outside pump. There were three outside buildings; the girls toilet, the boys toilet and the woodshed near the back of the school. A large stove was located in the northwest rear corner of the school. At the beginning of each school year the woodshed was full of wood and a large back-up supply was neatly stacked outside in front of the shed.

A one-room country school is a social experience as well as an educational one. Between ten and sixteen students were enrolled at The Little Red School; the number in each grade varied from time to time. I was the only one in my grade for all but a few months of my eight years at the school. In other words, I was simultaneously valedictorian and dunce of the class.

Each student was assigned specific duties each school week of the year. The duties were: carrying in the wood, cleaning the blackboards, cleaning the erasers, carrying in drinking water from the pump, filling the pail in the hall next to the wash basin with water, raising and lowering the flag each day and ringing the bell in the morning and at the end of each recess.

Recess was a time for playing softball, run-sheep-run, hide and seek, king of the mountain, and the winter snow game of fox and geese. Because of the paucity of students, big kids and little kids all played together. It was expected that the big kids would watch over the little kids. Once in a great while, in the spring of the year, two big kids from the wrong side of the tracks in New Lisbon would come to the schoolyard and threaten to beat up the big kids. The intruders often won this battle and returned victorious to New Lisbon.

Miss Niles

Catherine Niles boarded at our house. The price of her room and board was $16 per month. Her monthly salary was $85. Dad was chairman and a director of the school board. One of his jobs was to prepare Miss Niles' paycheck and have it signed by the treasurer before presenting it to her. I would often ride along with dad on this important mission.

Miss Niles was a saint in my eyes. She was a warm, loving and intelligent teacher who gently led me through those first four years of my education. She was also my speech therapist. I had a heavy Swedish accent when

I started school. My sister Mildred, who is four years older than me, always asked mom and dad to speak English when she came home from school. As a result, I was non lingual, speaking neither Swedish nor English well. Miss Niles would put me through speech drills repeating phrases like, "The chickens are in the chicken coop." I would repeat, "The shickens are in the shicken coooop." Then, in an effort to get the "CH" sound from me, she would have me imitate trains. After a perfect "CH" on the choo-choo exercise she once again would say, "Kenny, now say "The chickens are in the chicken coop." I would promptly say,

Miss Niles

"The shickens are in the schicken cooop." I got so I could imitate trains to perfection but was not as effective at learning to pronounce the "CH" sound. She kept working with me; I eventually got it.

I remember one cold winter evening, when I was in the fourth grade. Everyone in our house caught the flu except Miss Niles and me. I slept with her a couple of nights in her front bedroom since it was the only infection-free place in the house. Miss Niles shyly asked me not to mention this to anyone and I haven't until now. Although I have no idea why she asked me to keep it secret.

The spelling test

Once, I cheated in spelling. I was in the fourth grade. I always got 100 in spelling. But on this particular day I saw the correctly-spelled words on Miss Niles' desk and was shocked to see that I had misspelled the word "interest." I had spelled it "intrest." Noting the missing "e" between the "t" and the "r," I quickly inserted it before handing in my now-perfect paper. Life was living hell for me thereafter. I had never cheated before in my life and now my conscience was heavily burdened with this newly-committed sin. I carried this guilt with me for four months. I wasn't eating well; my normally cheerful demeanor disappeared and life just wasn't the same. Finally, in desperation, after a very long four months, I walked up to Miss Niles desk and quietly confessed my sin. I tearfully told her that I only deserved a 90 for that spelling test four months ago. Yes, I had cheated and was very sorry for it. Miss Niles saw how disturbed I was. Instead of chastising me, she gently put her arm around my shoulders and comforted me, thanking me for telling the truth. Then she reduced my spelling score in her grade book from 100 to 90 for that awful day four months prior to my confession. What a relief! I had just experienced a wonderful and memorable lesson in honesty. Miss Niles compassionate session proved to be the catharsis that set me straight again. I never again cheated in any test thereafter throughout my nineteen years of formal education.

Miss Niles retired from teaching the year I finished the fourth grade. That summer she asked me to visit her parents home with her in Mauston for a few days. We rowed down Lemonweir River in a rowboat and fished for bluegills and perch. What a wonderful, beautiful experience to enjoy the warm sun while the river's current lazily drifted us downstream among the cattails and swamp grass near the shore. We caught bluegills for supper that evening.

I knew I would miss Catherine Niles when I entered the fifth grade in September. I wondered how any teacher could ever replace her. Evelyn Evenson was her replacement. She taught at the Little Red School for two years. Miss Evenson was named well for she had an even temper and a cheerful disposition. My fifth and sixth grade years were uneventful.

Miss Hall

During my seventh and eighth grade years, Betty Hall was my teacher. Miss Hall was young, pleasant and easy-going, but she was incapable of understanding seventh and eighth grade math. Since I was the only one in my grade, she gave me the answer book to help me solve the problems. I enjoyed the experience of explaining to Miss Hall the mysteries of seventh and eighth grade math as we perused my completed work assignments together.

One day Miss Bergsdorff, the County Superintendent visited our school and left Miss Hall a pile of IQ tests. She asked Miss Hall to administer these tests and compute and chart the IQ of each child. Miss Hall didn't have a clue as to how to manage this task. She asked for my assistance. I enjoyed helping her through the tests. I conducted the tests and calculated each student's score. Miss Hall looked on in awe as I divided the "Educational Age" by the "Mental Age" and charted the scores on a graph. The scores were all sent to Miss Bergsdorff as requested. Some years later, Miss Bergsdorff commented to my sister that all the IQ records seemed to be in my handwriting. They were.

I was surprised to find that Everett Schultz approached the genius level on these test scores. Many farm boys would only go through the eighth grade and then back to the farm. I encouraged Everett to go on to high school when he finished grade school. He said he didn't expect to. He said he would work on the farm with his dad instead. My efforts to persuade him to attend high school failed. Everett stayed on the farm and eventually owned his own truck and became an independent truck driver.

War

It was Sunday afternoon, December 7, 1941 at about 3:00 p.m. We had our radio on. We heard President Roosevelt's speech informing of the Japanese attack on Pearl Harbor. World War II changed our lives. We had daylight savings time, gas rationing, food rationing, and our school year was shortened to end in May rather than June, enabling everyone to work in the fields at planting time.

Mom gave each of us half of our sugar ration in jars that were placed in front of our plates on the kitchen table. She used the other half of the sugar ration for cooking. Dad would sometimes buy part of my jar of sugar to sweeten his coffee when his jar was empty.

Some of the boys over 17 were deferred from the draft and stayed on the farm while others went off to war. We would occasionally see gold stars in the windows of some of the families; they had lost their sons to the ravages of war. We listened to the news, read the newspapers and studied maps of unknown places of the world that were now personalized by the presence there of our relatives, friends and neighbors. As a seventh grader, war seemed as unending and hopeless as grade school.

I finally finished the eighth grade in May of 1943 and looked forward to starting high school the next September.

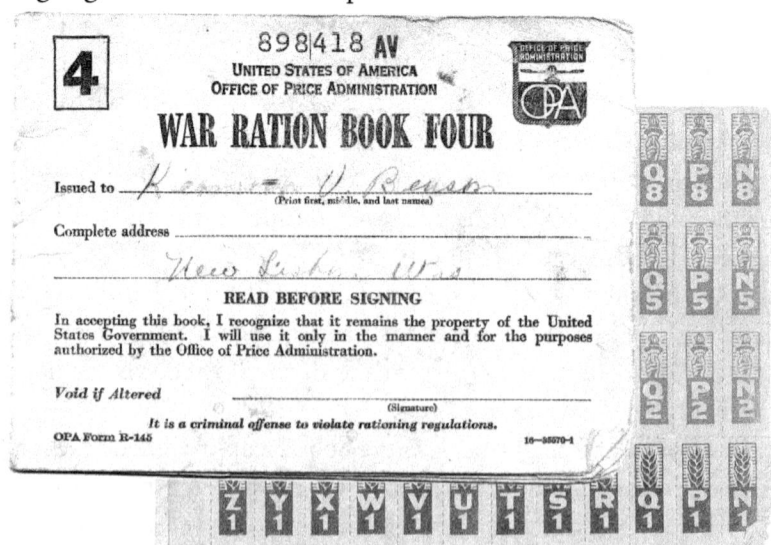

New Lisbon High School
In the summer of 1943, I started taking clarinet lessons at New Lisbon

The caption of this photo from the March 6, 1942, *Milwaukee Sentinel* read: "Turn pennies into dollars–Throughout the Badger Bomber campaign, Wisconsin's school children have saved their pennies and turned dollars into the fund to provide a Wisconsin warplane for America's airmen. Here are pupils of the "Little Red School House" at New Lisbon who raised $10 at a basket social this week, typical of many another classroom doing its bit." Ken is in the back row, third from the left.

High School. I was going to play in the high school band! I was excited about the prospects of beginning high school that next September.

I also decided to go out for football. I weighed about 140 pounds. I liked the idea of participating in sports, even though I had never seen a football game in my life nor listened to one on the radio. It didn't take long for me to realize that I was a total football illiterate on the practice field. Coach Arbin York would yell out, "grab legs!" I would, and hear him yell, "You can't grab legs on offense, Benson, what's the matter with you?" I realized that there really was no way to understand what a football game was all about in practice. It was not until I sat on the bench and viewed my very first football game, six weeks after the first practice, that it all started coming together.

Needless to say, I was the butt of many jokes because of my stupidity. I managed to letter in my sophomore year, played every minute of the football season in my junior year; I missed a minute and a half of season play in my senior year. That year, I was elected co-captain of the team.

Ken (#19, front row) was co-captain of the New Lisbon High School football team.

Receive High Honors At NLHS

KENNETH BENSON

Kenneth Benson will represent the senior class of New Lisbon high school as valedictorian at the commencement exercises to be held in the high school gymnasium Thursday evening, May 29, 1947.

Kenneth was a member of the band four years, its personnel director in his junior year and this year served as president of the band organization. He participated in football four years and Pep Club three years. He was treasurer of his junior class and vice president of this year's senior class.

From the New Lisbon Times, June, 1947

Al Grube's Childhood

Growing up in the City

Growing up in the 1930's and 1940's in Sheboygan, Wisconsin, life's pace was slow. Honesty and integrity were a given and the economic distance between families was not obvious. The people in our community were close to one another and tolerant of minor infractions of the rules.

Robbing the Cradle

My father, Al, owned a neighborhood drugstore. After a search for a dependable clerk, he hired Wanda Kaepernick, a girl from the neighborhood. She turned out to be a good worker with high personal ethics. One thing led to another and after a period of time, Al proposed to and married Wanda. At the time she was 21 and he was 45.

Because Al had a bad case of psoriasis from above his elbow to his wrists and didn't want to pass it on to his children, he announced he did not want children. But Wanda wanted to be a mother, so she sought the support of Dr. Squires, a personal friend, fellow hunter and a good prescribing physician for Al's pharmacy. Dr. Squires took Al aside and cautioned him that his refusal to have children could result in a lost mate.

When Al reached the age of 50, I was born. I'm sort of glad he changed his mind.

Celebrity Status is Nice

Once born, I became the eighth wonder of the world in my father's eyes. I was like a beloved toy. The salespeople who called on my father quickly discovered that a gift for me was a way to sell dad their wares.

I became the proud owner of a miniature football, miniature basketball, miniature baseball bat and many other gifts. The gift I remember most was a casting rod designed for a three year

Al's father's pharmacy. The second floor was our home, so there was always a pharmacist on the premises.

old. I kept that casting rod until I left home for the service in 1946.

Rex My Defender

My dad felt no boy's life would be complete without a dog. So, Rex moved into my life. Rex was a beautiful black and white English setter who immediately accepted his assignment as my protector.

His dog pen was a space the size of a one-car garage surrounded by an eight-foot high fence. One fine day a neighbor boy decided to beat me up. This was an unwise decision on his part because Rex leaped over the fence and convinced my attacker that running from the skirmish was a wise decision.

Rex's action prevented any other kid in the neighborhood from even considering beating me up. I was definitely hands off, period.

The Walking Threesome

Many fond memories are still very vivid. Rex, dad, and me, "just the boys." The dog had to be walked. I loved that time together with my dad, and he enjoyed these outings, too.

Dad was a great storyteller. Visiting with people who had known my father, they all spoke fondly of his storytelling abilities. I like to talk, but I don't believe I ever gained the stature among my friends that he had with his.

My life changed when my father died. He was only 59. I was 9 years old and couldn't understand why he had to leave us, a decision I now realize was not his to make. Unfortunately, my mother refused to let the doctors autopsy him. It was assumed that he died of a cerebral vascular accident, but we will never know.

Later on in life, my mother apologized to me profusely, because it was possible that the diagnosis could have been useful in protecting me from the same demise. Today it really makes no difference. We all must leave this

Al's mom and dad at the Chicago World's Fair in 1933. Their age difference is obvious.

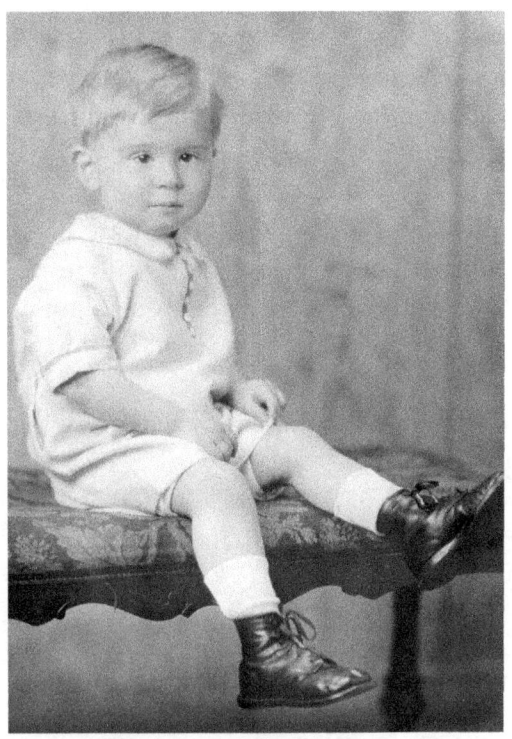

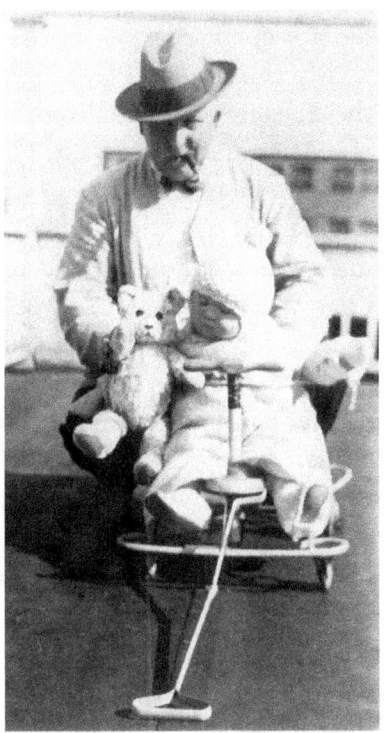

Innocence personified. My nickname, "Bud," was carried until my military days, 18 years later.

Al Senior and Junior. "No no Teddy" came along for the ride.

life for some reason. I have enjoyed my 79 years and I would like to continue, but when your time has come, it has come and you will not be able to change it.

My Mother Became My Sister

After dad died we moved in with my grandparents. Grandma and grandpa treated us more like brother and sister than mother and son. They seemed to pick up where they left off 13 years earlier when my mother married my father.

Unfortunately, a normal lifestyle in my grandparents home lasted only three months. One day in July, my mother got up early to scrub the kitchen floor. My grandmother also rose earlier than usual, marched across the wet floor, slipped and broke her hip.

The attending physician felt that the surgery required to set the hip would more than likely kill my grandmother, and he felt not to do it wouldn't delay her demise much more than a week anyway. So the doctors did not operate.

My grandmother lay in pain for twelve long years, five years longer than the advising physician lived! Every joint in her body calcified. Arthritis did not miss much of her body. Her hands and feet looked more like claws than the normal appendages.

The pain was intense and her prayers to die became almost an on going mantra. Grandma had to be turned almost every fifteen minutes 24 hours a day, seven days a week. My mother and grandfather rotated nights so they could turn her from side to belly to side to back right around the clock.

Her pain pills gave her some relief, but she had to take them every four hours. At times she begged for them more frequently. Her demise was actually a welcome event, yet each of us in our own way missed her terribly.

The Dueling Duet

By the time I reached 10 I became a bit argumentative. My grandfather, Ernst Kaepernick Sr., was a strong proponent of socialism and I believed in capitalism, so the arguments became loud, consistent, and trying for my mother. In fact, we disagreed so frequently and it upset my mother to the point where she decided to build a two-story home with two totally independent apartments.

The new home did reduce the arguments dramatically and mom regained her status of "mom" to a large extent. I did have twin beds in my room, however, so I had a guest—my grandfather appeared every other night—his night off from turning my grandmother. On those evenings, we never ar-

Mother. Wanda Grube in her 30s when she was widowed.

gued. Looking back that does seem odd.

I Wasn't Goody-Goody Two Shoes

In today's world some of my stunts might have cost me prison time, a fine or probation. In my case I just upset our neighbors and my punishment was a tongue lashing from my mother.

Our neighbor to the north was a jerk in my opinion. He sold and stocked potato chips in local retail stores.

He had a way of being a bit pompous and in an effort to bring him down to a more tolerable size, my friends and I blocked the two doorways of his home with accumulated junk from a recent city trash collection. Then we telephoned him and informed him we would let the air out of his truck tires.

Ernst Kaepernick, Sr. My grandfather was a cabinet maker by profession. Today I prize a chair and a dresser in my own home, both made by Ernst almost 100 years earlier.

We removed the stems from the tire valves and took off. By the time he got out of his front door, he had four flat tires. Needless to say, he was displeased. We made a conscious effort to remain out of sight for a week. He did communicate with my mom, and I did promise never to do that again. It was a dumb idea!

Turning over the shed owned by our neighbor to the west wasn't a very nice thing to do, either. We were suspects, but we did it in the darkness of night without forewarning, so we never were accused. I'm glad we grew out of this rowdy behavior before we got into real trouble.

Grandpa Was Bright!

When I left for military service the first time in 1946, I can remember saying to my mother, "Grandpa has to be the stupidest human being alive."

Two years later, I was granted a 30-day convalescent furlough after hernia surgery and I hitchhiked home from California to visit my mom and grandfather. My visit was not pre-announced, so I came through the backyard to find my grandfather hanging out sheets on the second floor balcony. When he saw me he became so excited he almost jumped from the second story to give me a welcome home hug. After having lived with him for nine years, I discovered for the first time that he really loved me. A very surprising turn of events. During the following weeks I had another epiphany. As I was leaving for my return trip to California, I heard myself say to my mom, "Has grandpa been studying day and night since I left. He sure has learned a lot in the last two years!"

No Free Ride

Money and work were synonymous in my life. I never asked for money. If I wanted money I earned it. As soon as I could, I got a paper route. I tried to become the Sunday paper mogul. Most routes at the time were 40 to 50 papers. A Catholic friend of mine, Jimmy Fassbender, and I combined forces. He would go to early mass, so I carried most of the papers since my church had a late service. Jimmy collected most of the payments. By the time we moved on to other projects we were serving about 180 customers covering a good share of Sheboygan's south side.

From Sunday papers I went to working in a drugstore, where I served as soda jerk, stock boy, errand boy, and sales clerk when needed.

I loved the work, which came quite naturally, but the boss, who was an actor first and a pharmacist second, was always fun to be around. He was also very understanding about mistakes.

One day I was asked to fetch a gallon of butterscotch topping for the soda fountain. It was in the back room storage on the top shelf. Tiptoes and fingertips brought it in reach, but just. I did short jumps to move it to the edge of the shelf where I hoped to have it drop into my extended arms. What I wasn't aware of was that it was partially open and it tipped, spilling the butterscotch over my head as it fell. "No, no, it was for ice cream sundaes, not a Butterscotch Bud!" George Fessler commented.

I did clean up, but I had to go back home and change into clean, dry, un-butterscotched clothes.

For the rest of my future career, I avoided soda fountains like the plague.

Bud the trumpeter. I tried hard, even taking band in high school, but I just had no talent.

Maybe He Knew

In the Sheboygan school system the students were divided into three groups: kindergarten to 6th grade, 7th to 9th grades (junior high), and 10th through 12th grades (senior high).

When I graduated from Urban Junior High School and prepared to enter Central High School, my registration day was a bit traumatic. As I attempted to register, I was told I must first go to the principal's office to personally receive authorization from the Principal, George Menas. Not the vice-principal, but the top man himself. This was of real concern to me, because I did not see this as a welcome event.

As instructed, I approached the principal's secretary, informed her that I was to see Mr. Menas before I would be allowed to register, and then stood and shook with concern. For some reason I had been singled out as a troublemaker. The secretary escorted me to into Mr. Menas' huge office, introduced me, and promptly left us alone.

"Alfred Grube, your reputation for creating problems has preceded you. You and your gang created problems at Urban which we will absolutely not tolerate at Central High. One incident of any kind and I will personally see that you are expelled–any questions?"

My reply was, "Sir, I do not have a gang, I am not a gang leader, and I assure you I will try to avoid misdeeds at all costs."

His retort, "You are excused. You may register and good luck on your promise!"

Almost Made Two Years

Harry Berg, a good friend who was a senior and ready to graduate, decided that I should be the all-school president in my senior year. He insisted he would run my campaign for this esteemed position. He seemed to be politically savvy, and even though I was a long way from being an intellectual, my classmates felt I was nice and fun to be around. Since I had been free of misdeeds, my early reputation did not become an issue.

As the final act before the election, each candidate was required to make a plea for the student body's support. I had to face 1,200 of my fellow students and ask for their vote. I was the last to speak, and my campaign manager, Harry, had coached me to emphasize there issues that the student body was concerned about but were in limbo. The administration had failed to act on them.

Principal Menas chose to skip the speeches and was obvious in his absence. I was glad. What I wasn't aware of is his office was able to listen into the presentations being given in the auditorium. My speech went from a reasonable plea for the student body's vote to a challenge that school administration was withholding decisions on the students requests. As I pounded on the podium, shouting that our requests were resting, resting, resting on the desks of the principals of North and Central, Mr. Menas flew into the auditorium. He was red-faced and furious.

I was elected all-school president much to the chagrin of Principal Menas. I did serve reasonably and was even complimented at the end of the first semester. But I decided not to run for re-election in the second semester which historically had been won by the incumbent.

Instead, I ran for class valedictorian. Harry wasn't there to help me and a united faculty working against me insured my defeat. Incidentally, it was the last time the valedictorian and salutatorian were elected by the students. Ever since, they have been selected by the faculty based on grade point average. I agree with that approach.

First Semester Officers

| James Grasse | Don Herman | Carol Debrauske | Alfred Grube |
| Treasurer | Secretary | Vice-President | President |

College: Ken Benson

UW-Madison Business School

1947 was the year I slipped from the lofty position of valedictorian of my New Lisbon High School class to a bewildered and confused freshman on the huge University of Wisconsin-Madison campus of twenty thousand students.

One of my poorest decisions in life was to accelerate my studies because of lack of money. I completed the requirements for my undergraduate degree in three and one-half years. I also worked more than thirty hours each week. In other words, there was absolutely no time for me to fully enjoy extra-curricular activities or make new friends; it was almost all work and study and no play.

I entered the University in the fall of 1947 and graduated in January, 1951, with a Bachelor of Business degree. After a stint in the service, I returned to the University of Wisconsin-Madison and entered Law School. I graduated in June, 1957, with a Bachelor of Law Degree, later designated Doctor, Jurisprudence.

The Janitor

Working as a part-time janitor at Chadbourne Hall changed my life. Chadbourne Hall was the oldest girls dormitory on the University of Wisconsin campus. Located at the corner of Park and University Avenues, it was named after an early UW dignitary who, ironically, was opposed to women studying at the University.

I planned to supplement my meager life savings of $1,200 by working as a janitor, thus enabling me to complete my undergraduate studies. The pay was seventy cents per hour. I often worked thirty-five hours a week. My duties varied. I scrubbed floors, washed walls, washed windows, changed light bulbs, moved furniture, baled waste paper or anything else Mike asked me to do. Mike, a short Czechoslovakian immigrant was the head janitor and my boss. Chet Hood was the manager of the dormitory. Miss Schoenfelt was the dietician. Miss Morgan was the housemother.

Bill was my co-worker my freshman year. He was a World War II veteran. We worked well together. He would often take a cigarette break. He would offer me cigarettes; I would refuse. Each day that he would take a break the same ritual occurred; except one day I took him up on his offer and smoked my first cigarette. From then on I would accept the offer of a free smoke. It wasn't long before I was asking him for a cigarette. Finally I was so embarrassed about my freeloading that I began buying my own cartons of Lucky Strikes.

I also washed the windows at Barnard Hall, a four-story girls dorm adjacent to Chadbourne. One sunny autumn day, Mike asked me to wash both the inside and the outside of the fourth floor windows at Barnard. Crawling awkwardly through each open window to wash it outside, then back through the window again to wash it inside, seemed inefficient to me. Instead, I crawled out on the fourth floor ledge of the outside of the building, along with my window washing gear, and walked carefully down the ten-inch ledge, washing the outside of all the windows, before crawling back into the building to wash them on the inside. I was pleased with my efficient progress. My self-congratulations were abruptly interrupted by an urgent summons to come down to Mr. Hood's office immediately!

It turned out that a member of the Board of Regents was driving down University Avenue. He was shocked as he looked up and saw me on the fourth floor ledge. He abruptly turned his car around, parked it at Chadbourne, ran into Mr. Hood's office, exclaiming that some idiot window washer was walking the ledge of Barnard Hall and that Mr. Hood had better get him off from there in a hurry! Chet Hood blanched; he quickly sent word to get me down to his office immediately! That was the end of efficient fourth-floor window washing at Barnard.

A Crack in the Ceiling

I was a trusted employee. I had been a part-time janitor for more than three years, I no longer yelled "man on floor" as I pursued my janitorial duties. I carried a master key that opened every dormitory room in both Chadbourne and Barnard Halls, meaning that I had access to more than three hundred girls rooms. I was too naive to comprehend the significance of this fact. Selling duplicate keys to interested male students could have easily richly supplemented the seventy cents an hour that I was paid for my labors. The thought of starting this enterprise never occurred to me. Yet if it had, a short walk to the hardware store for key duplication would have put me in business. I am thankful for my naivety; it kept me from being expelled from the University of Wisconsin.

In my third year at Chadbourne, two other students were hired for part-time janitor work. They only worked on Saturdays. I became suspicious of their work when I noticed that about 7:00 a.m. and an hour or two thereafter, the freight elevator was parked on the fifth attic floor of the building. I went up to investigate. The two students sheepishly crawled out of the attic.

"What are you guys doing, anyway?" I asked.

"Didn't you know?"

"About what?"

Then they proceeded to lead me into the attic crawl space, pointing to a large crack through the ceiling, immediately above the girls' shower. They had been watching the girls morning showers on fourth floor. I suggested that they should forget about their discovery and get back to work. No doubt this crack was punched through the ceiling above the showers shortly after the building was constructed in the late 1800s; young ladies showering had possibly been viewed from this crawl space for more than seventy-five years.

Sally

I quit my janitor job during my senior year at the UW. I began driving a truck to deliver laundry, bakery goods, towels and sheets throughout the campus to dorms, restaurants, athletic facilities and the university president's home. The pay was the same; but I had a reason for the change. I began dating Sally Drewry and was about to ask her to marry me. Sally lived in room A-6 on the first floor of Chadbourne Hall. Miss Morgan was thrilled the night Sally displayed the sparkling one-quarter carat diamond on her finger to her. She had always been our friend and was aware of our courtship.

I turned in my master key, never having violated the trust bestowed upon me.

Summer Work

With only one semester remaining before my graduation from the University of Wisconsin in January of 1951, I decided to spend the summer of 1950 living at my parents' small farm home, nestled among the sandstone bluffs three miles west of New Lisbon, Wisconsin.

My summer job was factory laborer at the Walker Company in New Lisbon, a manufacturer of large steel and stainless steel tanks for the dairy and paper industry. The work was dirty, boring and dangerous. I hated it. I think Bob Walker, owner and CEO, feared that I might become a union organizer. He transferred me to his home to assist in building a garage in his backyard. Mr. Foley, a high school industrial arts teacher, was hired by Bob to construct the garage. He knew little about garage construction and

I knew even less. For two weeks I helped Mr. Foley build Bob's garage. Finally, I threw up my arms in despair and quit the Walker job. The ugly, badly-constructed garage remained in Bob's backyard for years. Whenever I drove past this miserable building I was tempted to level it in the hope that it would forever be erased from my memory.

I did not reveal my dissatisfaction to Bob when I left; we seemed to be on good terms. This was confirmed in 1956 when Bob tried to hire me as an executive at Walker Company. I was completing my second year of law school. He suggested that I quit law school and begin working for him at a starting salary of $25,000 per year. The pay sounded attractive but I turned it down. Bob had three sons in the business and my summer job experience lingered in my mind.

Following the Wheat Harvest

A few days after leaving Walker Company in 1950, I hopped a bus for Aberdeen, South Dakota. My goal was to follow the wheat harvest. I remembered hearing Axel Jensen, our former hired man, speaking glowingly of harvesting wheat in South Dakota. Upon arriving in Aberdeen, I discovered that the summer's poor crop of wheat had already been harvested. I checked into the YMCA.

Early the next morning, I stood in line at the Aberdeen employment office. By mid-morning I found a job unloading plumbing fixtures from a boxcar located on a railroad siding next to the local Crane plumbing distributor. It was hot outside; inside the boxcar it was stifling. After I finished unloading the boxcar, I walked into the Crane distributor's warehouse and began helping fill orders for local plumbers. I spent the next three days doing this work. The next morning, August 2, 1950 was my 21st birthday. I had just finished eating breakfast at a local restaurant. I walked up to the counter to pay my bill, when the owner of the Crane distributorship walked up to the counter, grabbed my bill and said, "you can work for us as long as you wish."

I worked another week. It was payday. After receiving my paycheck for my 80 hours at Crane at $1.58 per hour, I told my boss I would be leaving Aberdeen for Grand Fork to follow the wheat harvest.

I checked out of the Aberdeen YMCA. Dick Olson, A University of North Dakota student was also checking out to hitchhike back to his parent's home in Grand Forks. We decided to hitchhike there together. The journey was slow and tiring. We finally successfully thumbed a ride that evening with three men who seemed a little drunk. The driver was reckless, often hitting the shoulder of the road. He drove at a high rate of speed. Dick and I were relieved to arrive safely in Grand Forks about midnight. I stayed at Dick's home until Monday morning. Once again, I stood in line at the employment office. This time the wheat crop in the Grand Forks area was thriving, but it was green and wouldn't be ready to harvest until another three weeks. I found a job stacking hay and helping a farmer install a barbed wire fence around his pasture on his small farm in the Red River Valley, just a few miles outside of Grand Forks.

The farmer and his wife were very friendly. I slept in a woodshed near the house. I carried two books with me; a book of Irish Plays and a Bible. I tried to understand the plays and prayed that I might learn to pray.

We started work early each morning after eating a hearty breakfast. We had a mid-morning coffee break, ate noon dinner together, had a snack break in mid-afternoon and then supper in the evening. Hard work and five meals a day! We built fence when the hay in the field was drying and hauled hay and stacked it after it was cured.

An Offer from J. C. Penney

My farm work was completed in four days and after supper on this last day of work, I leafed through the Grand Forks daily newspaper. The headline story revealed the arrival the next day of Mr. J.C. Penney to visit his Grand Forks store.

Early the next morning, I laid out on my woodshed cot the one set of dress clothes I had packed in my suitcase. I dressed up in my white shirt, brown print tie and glen plaid, single-breasted suit and asked the farmer to drive me to the Penney store in Grand Forks.

There, I shook hands with J.C. Penney himself! His Minneapolis district manager was at his side. I chatted with Mr. Penney and explained that I had worked part-time in his Madison Penney store while attending the University of Wisconsin. I also told him that I had only one semester remaining toward my degree in marketing and merchandising. He turned to his district manager, pointing to me and exclaimed, "Hire this man." Although the job would have been that of any other beginning trainee, I was pleased to have the top man in the organization offer me the job. I never took them up on the offer because Uncle Sam made a more pressing offer of $72 per month when I graduated in January of 1951.

My work in Grand Forks finished, I began my long trip hitch-hiking back to New Lisbon. My first ride took me 80 miles east on U. S. Highway 2 to a lonely intersection. I stood for eight hours on the desolate road without anyone stopping. Finally, late in the afternoon, a man and his young son picked me up. He was driving a 1950 Nash. As we drove at the hair-raising speed of 105 miles per hour, he explained that he had been delayed three days because he had hit a deer and the car had to be repaired. The car would vibrate when traveling 95, but smoothed out as it passed the 100 mark. I was uneasy as we sped toward New Lisbon, but the trip took less than six hours and I arrived safely home.

Building Silos

I needed money. I boarded a Greyhound bus to Madison and found a job with the Madison Silo Company, repairing and building silos. I began work on an extension and repair crew. We would remove the silo roof, extend the height of the silo, put a new roof back on and then swing around the outside of the silo on a boatman's chair, pointing the now taller and newly roofed silo with concrete wherever needed.

A few days later, I joined a three-man building crew, replacing an injured man who had been struck on his arm by a broken piece of a concrete stay while standing on the ground near the silo. The crew traveled from farm to farm, building silos on poured concrete pads previously installed by another team. The farmer provided food and lodging. If it was a corporate farm we stayed in a hotel and ate in restaurants. We each consumed double meals to keep up with the calories we burned each day.

We worked from dawn until dark, completing the average sized forty-foot silo in a day and a half. This was a piecework job. The foreman of the crew received three cents a stay and was responsible for building a level and sturdy silo. If he failed, he had to rebuild it at his own expense. We, non-risk takers were paid 1.5 cents for each 67-pound, grooved stay we nested into place.

We stood on movable scaffolding inside the silo, jacking it higher after each round of concrete stays were in place. Each stay was lifted by a gasoline engine-powered hoist. The two on the scaffold would catch the heavy stay as it reached the top then fit it into place until the circumference of each round of the silo was complete.

After completing round upon round of stays we would end up standing on the inside scaffold at the very top of the completed silo. Steel hoops were bolted around each round of stays as the silo grew in height. Then, an aluminum roof was installed and the interior of the silo coated by whisk-broom with a light slurry mix of water, cement and sand.

I helped build several silos in southern Wisconsin and Northern Illinois. This completed my 1950 summer work and in mid-September I enrolled for my final semester at the University of Wisconsin in Madison.

Ken (front row, third from left) poses with student and faculty members of the University of Wisconsin School of Commerce School Council in 1950.

College: Al Grube

University of Wisconsin Pharmacy School

In 1948, as my first hitch in the military was drawing to a close, my letters to my mother were filled with the idea I was going to go out east to pharmacy school. I had selected the Philadelphia College of Pharmacy and Science.

Why would I even consider going out of state? Well, one of my former employers was an alumni and bragged about the school whenever our paths crossed. He reached the hard sell point when I left his employ. His words rang in my ears and I decided that was for me.

My mom wanted me to go to the University of Wisconsin. As my grandmother's health deteriorated, my mom's pleas became more intense until I conceded I would enroll at the UW and transfer after two years. Once at Wisconsin, I realized that I was happy there. Wisconsin had a good reputation and my love for the school and faculty grew with each passing week.

College Turned Into A Challenge

I was not an exemplary student in high school, so I was required to take entrance exams to officially enroll in UW-Madison. I had to take a four-hour exam with no smoking permitted. This really tested my metal. After the first half hour I began to suffer withdrawal symptoms. I completed the exam and my grades were sufficient to allow me to enter the university.

I decided I would quit smoking cigarettes and smoke a pipe or cigars only. It was a challenging decision, but it was a wise start.

Because of my military service from 1946 to 1948, I qualified for the GI bill, which was a godsend. Between the GI bill and a part-time job, I had just enough to struggle through a four-year program to graduation. The 1950's spawned a different type of college student. Everyone did not come from the higher income families. Many of the students were ex-GIs who brought with them more life experiences and a positive desire to learn. It was a competitive environment.

Grade Point Needed

Being away from academia for a couple years really doesn't seem like much, but when you're in that position you discover you have forgotten a lot. It becomes harder to digest large sums of information and be able to regurgitate it at the blink of an eye.

My first semester at the University proved to me that I could not hold a candle to my younger classmates. Among other problems, I was unable to both party and study hard enough to pass my courses. At the end of my first semester, I had a grade point of 0.82, not sufficient. I was now on probation. One more performance like that and I would be gone.

My motivation to do better was intense. To be kicked out of school would crush my vision and my hope of owning a drugstore would never materialize. I worked very hard and suffered lots of pain, but I did end up with a 1.5 grade point. On a three-point scale, I had a B average.

To improve my standing I went to summer school and got all A's and didn't have a lot of fun. My success was due to Bob Keller, my roommate, who incidentally became a practicing physician in Sheboygan years later. I learned how to study and graduated with a B+ average.

Don't Share Your Experiences Until You Know Your Listeners

I requested and received the right to live in the men's dorms at the University. Ochsner House was the home of my Sheboygan buddy, Harry Berg, and to be around him was a trip unto itself.

When I moved into the house, I was escorted by an upperclassman to my room on the fourth floor. As we entered the house there was a water fight in progress. The students were soaking towels and washcloths in the sink and then tossing them at one another.

My mentor saw that I had a look of disdain on my face, and asked if I didn't think this would be great fun to participate in. I informed him that I had just been discharged from the service and having been a sergeant with a degree of responsibility and trust, I found this activity very childish. Disgusting, actually.

After this outpouring of sentiment, my mentor proceeded to introduce me to my peers: "Sergeant, I'd like you to meet Lieutenant So and So, Captain So and So, Major So and So, and Colonel So and So." I never again mentioned my rank or my previous military service.

I was surrounded with heroes who had served with distinction in World War II. I was a Johnny-Come-Lately, serving after the shooting had stopped. They all participated in the actual battle and several carried scars from their service to our country.

A Deal with the ROTC

I had found a home at the UW, but in 1951 at the beginning of the second semester of my sophomore year, the Korean War led to a call-up of reservists. I didn't want to lose the sergeant stripes I earned in my first enlistment just after WWII, so I joined the reserves.

I sought out the person in charge of the ROTC program at the university in the hope I could join the ROTC and be able to finish my pharmacy program. He assured me that with two years of previous active duty, I could enroll immediately in ROTC, begin my training as a first-semester junior and receive a two-year deferment until I graduated. At the end of my senior year I would have several months before I would be called up. This would give me time to take my Wisconsin State Pharmacy Boards. I would then enter the service as a second lieutenant. I signed up so fast you wouldn't believe it. I would not, and now could not leave the University of Wisconsin, and so be it. I was happy to stay.

Answer Fast. It Can Help

The comprehensive Wisconsin State Board Pharmacy exam had three sections. The first was a written exam that covered all the highlights of my coursework. It was extensive, but reasonable and fair.

The second section, a practical test, required making eight to ten compounds. Your efforts were monitored as you proceeded. Compounding, or making the products yourself, has certainly decreased over the years, but it is the one way you can adjust a medicine to the person's size, weight, age, or physical condition.

For the third part, each contestant was interviewed by a member of the State Board of Pharmacy. He (as there were no women on the board at that time) could ask any question he felt was pertinent. My challenger asked a number of questions in rapid succession and all over the block. I did my best to answer the questions faster than he asked me. After five or six questions, he relaxed and just shot the breeze. I concluded my fast, crisp answers convinced him I was worthy of licensure and so I passed the whole three-day ordeal with flying colors and received my pharmacy license a week later.

Now, more than 50 years later, I still carry an active, validated license. And I carry that with pride, even though I will probably never practice again.

My advice, whenever you are questioned in an exam format, always answer a little faster than you were asked!

Ken Benson's Military Service

A "crew-cut" Benson stands in front of the barracks at Camp Stoneman in July, 1951.

Below decks on the SS Brewster. Nineteen days of living like this made people seem overbearing unless you managed to discover just one little vacant spot where you could have some privacy.

Army Private, psywar

After working my way through college, I was disappointed with the pay of my first job. So, only two weeks after receiving my Bachelor of Business Administration degree from the University of Wisconsin, I signed a contract for a new job by enlisting in the Army for a draftee's term. I did not have the opportunity to negotiate my seventy-two dollars per month salary as an Army private. I was assigned to a new psychological warfare unit, First Radio Broadcasting and Leaflet Group in Ft. Riley, Kansas.

Tokyo

Sally and I were married on June 23, 1951, and, one month later on July 19, 1951, I was shipped overseas. On August 7, after sailing the Pacific Ocean for nineteen days on the U.S.S. Brewster, my unit docked in Yokohama Harbor, Japan.

I was stationed in downtown Tokyo. My unit lived in the Finance Building located among the government buildings in Tokyo. I wrote news commentaries at the Empire House office building located across the moat surrounding the emperor's palace. I also assisted in producing the evening broadcast to Korea and China of news and dramatic shows. We employed some of the top radio talent of Korea and China. We broadcast from Studio 19, Radio Tokyo, under the call sign, "The Voice of the United Nations Command." We transmitted at a power of 100,000 kilowatts, twice the power permitted in USA at that time. This was the same studio where Tokyo Rose made Japanese propaganda broadcasts to U.S. Troops during World War II.

Korea

On November 7, 1951 I was transferred to Pusan, Korea to write and produce the radio farm program "Your Farm Hour" that was eventually broadcast twice a week throughout South Korea. For a time, I also wrote seven children's stories per week for the "Your Story Grandmother" radio program. I also periodically traveled throughout South Korea taping on-the-spot news stories covering everything from Boy Scout Jamborees to prison camp riots. About ten of us were located on a hill overlooking the city in a small compound next to Radio Pusan. I spent ten months in Pusan. Some of these taped news stories were forwarded to Tokyo for broadcast to North Korea and China.

Pusan, Korea, December 1951. Ken's blonde mustache has started to grow, but he wrote that "Korea seems to have the ability of making my hairline move steadily backwards."

On May 23, 1952 I flew to Tokyo for two weeks to assist in producing radio programs that were to be broadcast to China. I had previously assisted in recording interviews with Chinese prisoners-of-war in a prison camp located on the island of Chejudou, about 100 miles south of Pusan. I was asked to help edit these interviews for broadcast from Radio Tokyo to Communist China. I also presented some ideas that I had about the growth of 4-H clubs in Korea.

The Hermes Typewriter

From letters written by Ken to Sally: Tuesday, May 26, 1952: "By the way honey, I've rented a Swiss typewriter called a Hermes 2000 that I'm doing all my work with and it is one of the sweetest little portables I have ever used. It has even more features than a stateside upright, but I still haven't decided whether I will buy it or not as it will cost me $100. I'm almost tempted to buy it anyway, for the darn thing is tremendous. It is built for good typing and seems to be sturdier than American portables. I'll keep using the machine this week and look around to see if I can get any American portables.

Radio new writers prepare scripts for broadcast on KBS, Pusan. Standing: Eddie Deerfield. Seated: Bill Morton, Ken Benson (back to camera) and Joe Dabney.

If I can't find any pretty soon, I'll buy this one, for I have to have a personal typewriter in civilian life anyway, and this will really help me out in Korea."

Saturday, May 31, 1952: "I have been working on a 4-H report all morning, and I am enclosing a carbon of some of the work I have been doing to give you a little idea what my main mission in Tokyo is on this tour. You know, I'm so in love with this Swiss typewriter that I've decided to buy it. I don't know what I'd do without it as it seems that I've been spoiled by the machine and take it with me almost everyplace I go. I've yet to find anything, portable or upright that compared with this little 'Hermes 2000'.

Monday, June 2, 1952: "I bought this little Swiss machine honey, for it is by far the greatest machine I have ever used and I don't feel I can get along without it. The thing really pounds along like a dream and now I can take my own typewriter with me wherever I go and get my work done."

Except for my first semester handwritten law exams at the University of Wisconsin Law School, I typed all exams with my Hermes 2000. After graduating from law school in June of 1957, John Day, a classmate of mine, and I opened the Law Office of Benson & Day in Marshfield, Wisconsin. My Hermes 2000 was the only typewriter in our office. On February 2, 1959 I began my career at Kohler Co. as a lawyer in the legal department. I didn't take my Hermes 2000 to the office, but I did use it for confidential memos written at home.

The Memories Return

The following was written by Ken for a 50th anniversary memory book about his unit in Korea:

• I remember recording statements from POWs. I eventually used them in a radio broadcast from Tokyo to China.

• In July of 1952, I moved from the small compound at the radio station in Pusan (which we all lovingly named "Paradise Pines R&R for GHQ") to the transmitter site which was about a ten-mile ride from the radio station. I went swimming every morning and used my rubber mattress to ride the surf until it hit a rock and blew up.

• Bill Wilson arrived in Korea on August 18, 1952, to replace me at Radio Korea. I returned to Tokyo after traveling from Pusan to Seoul by train with Bill for a few days of indoctrination. I had persuaded Bill to come over to replace me so I could meet my wife, Sally, who was sailing to Tokyo.

I emphasized how safe it was. Unfortunately, on that first train trip at about 2 a.m., guerrillas started shooting at our train from the mountains of Taejon. The MPs came through our car and shouted, "hit the floor!"

Bill and I were facing each other as prone as two soldiers could be, when he uttered to me, "safe, huh?" We traveled to Seoul without further incidents. I returned to Tokyo a few days later.

• Lt. Bill Eilers spent most of his time in Korea. Bill, a sensitive and soft-spoken man, worked very hard at grinding out the work for broadcast on Radio Pusan. Bill was everybody's friend and very sensitive to the Korean culture.

I remember the time when there was a love triangle murder-suicide outside our tent by two South Korean soldiers. It was mistakenly thought to be an attack from the outside. Capt. Leadley took immediate charge of the situation and set up all twelve of our outfit as a firing line, with our carbines pointed at a South Korean army unit of about 7000 men.

As Bill Eilers plopped down next to me, his gun fired and a bullet whizzed past my ear. Bill said, "Oops!" I exclaimed, "Oops, what the hell are you talking about? You damned near killed me!" We managed to set things straight with

Recording statements from Chinese POWs. Ken Benson eventually incorporated the interviews into a radio program broadcast from Tokyo to China. Seated at the table are Lt. Sing (dark glasses), Mr. Lieng (back to picture), and the Chinese POW at the mike (wearing cap). In the background, Sol Gamis operates the recorder. Another prisoner is near Sol.

Capt. Leadley before we turned our attention to war with our South Korean friends.

Sally Benson's memories of Japan

The following was written by Sally Benson for a 50th anniversary memory book about Ken's unit in Korea: Ken and I had been separated for 16 months. We were married on June 23, 1951. It was mid-October of 1952 when I finally sailed into Yokohama harbor on the President Lines' "President Wilson." We had spent all of our $525 savings for this one-way ticket to Japan. Ken said that the army wouldn't leave a corporal's wife standing alone in Tokyo if she had no way to return to the states. My father was not impressed.

Ken boarded the ship to greet me. He had arranged with a driver for one of the officers at 1st RB&L to drive him to the dock and back to Tokyo. We had an elegant breakfast together on the ship. After breakfast we gathered my luggage and hopped into the backseat of the OD 1951 Chevrolet and the driver headed for Tokyo.

We embraced; Ken kissed me, passionately of course. Immediately a

Sally is surrounded by Japanese children in Assagaya.

red light flashed behind us to the tune of a MP siren as we were pulled to the side of the road. The MP sternly warned Corporal Ken about the rules against necking in a military vehicle and waved us on.

Living in Japan was a great adventure. We rented two rooms in the servant's quarters of a former prince's palace in Assagaya. It was pink and managed by Mr. Pine, a Korean. We called it Pine's Pink Palace. The other eight wives in the palace were officer's wives. We all shared the kitchen, dining room and living room The only room really collectively used was the kitchen.

In December, 1952, there was a gas strike in Tokyo. The cold, damp climate of Tokyo chilled us to the bone, so Ken and I would take the train to the Onsan steam bath. First we took a steam bath, then a tub soak, then a rub-down. This included a delicate walk up and down Ken's back by a bikini-clad masseuse. The girls giggled when they looked at me, a tall blonde American, in the hot tub. They beckoned their friends from rooms down the hall to our room to view my legs. They gently pulled my leg out of the tub as they all exclaimed, "oh, stikinay!" (wonderful).

Glowing from the absorbed heat, we would hop the train for Assagaya, returning to our cold, corporal's servant quarters in Pine's Pink Palace. We bought an Hibachi to keep warm. Here we often entertained our guests as we sat on the tatami floor around the warm glow of the charcoal.

We toured Mt. Fuji, Nikko and Kyoto. I also visited Shimizu City. I loved exploring Tokyo and especially Christmas shopping on the Ginza.

Late in December, 1952, Ken and I boarded the troop ship, Thomas O'Hare, for Seattle. Ken had purchased a $20 space-available ticket for me. Our accommodations were of equal value. We arrived in Seattle on January 3, 1953, after two weeks of stormy seas.

Ken was discharged from the Army at Ft. Lewis, Washington, on January 6, 1953.

Al Grube's Military Service

Underage, Undersized

My friend's father owned a liquor store and a beer distributorship. He found a place for me on their staff. Unloading and loading trucks and delivery vehicles was a physical challenge for a five foot plus kid. Everything from cases of beer to half-barrels were all part of the job, and I did it.

When I tried to enlist in the Navy, my physical indicated I had a hernia. This would need to be repaired before I could enlist. It was repaired, but not in time to beat the closure date of the minority cruise program. The program was open to 17 and 18 year-olds and lasted until you turned 21. Instead, a six-year enlistment would be required. My response, "I'll join the Army for two years."

Two years service just after World War II was enough to qualify for the GI bill. This paid for my college undergraduate education. I enlisted just in time to qualify for full benefits. I wish that program could be continued, because it is a real help to those whose families do not have the money to give their kids a college education.

The Worst Thing That Can Happen is You Will Hear "No."

When I enlisted, I hoped I would wind up a medic. After basic training, I found myself not in the medics, but in ordinance where people do things with their hands using tools. If you'd have asked me what a screwdriver was I would have told you it was a cocktail; so much for being a do-it-yourselfer.

I was sent to Aberdeen Proving Grounds in Maryland to learn how to fix the control mechanisms on anti-aircraft guns. After sixteen weeks of intensive training, I became fully qualified. My orders were to go to Japan. I was sent to Camp Stoneman near Oakland, California, where paperwork was processed for GIs returning from and going to the far east.

It was my bad fortune to have studied typing in high school. This qualified me to be assigned to Camp Stoneman's replacement depot to assist in the processing of returning GI's who were leaving military service. My duties alternated between stretches of 24 to 48 hours of work around the clock, to stretches of time sitting and waiting for the next ship load of returnees to arrive. I was bored.

Risk Taking Came To An End

My stay at Camp Stoneman was not all bad. We had opportunities to travel around the area. One such trip was to visit Yosemite National Park, a beautiful place which could have been responsible for my early demise.

One could assume that built into my youth was a lack of fear, or maybe it was a lack of brains. For, traveling through the park, I observed a rock jutting out of the side of a small mountain. It was an idyllic lookout with wooden rails to protect the viewer from tumbling down the mountain.

I decided that a picture of myself lying on that rock with one leg in the air would be of interest to my friends and family. So I went around the barrier, crawled out on the rock, put one leg in the air and had my photograph taken by my traveling companion. The shot was well done, but as I tried to crawl back to land, I slipped and found myself dangling from the rock! An older lady fainted as I righted myself and crawled to safety. A 1,200-foot fall would probably be my last trip. I can understand the lady's concern, and I apologized to the group for the foolish stunt. As I thought about it, I decided I would not participate in any future grandstanding. It was far too risky.

Al Grube on the ledge at Yosemite. Can you imagine falling to the ground below?

It's a Small World

I decided to try to get an assignment away from the tedium of Camp Stoneman. Ask and it may be given to you! So I asked. I went to the Presidio in San Francisco, the port that handled troop movements to and from the Orient. I walked into the office of the person responsible for assigning GI's to serve on ships. I was greeted by the receptionist with a very loud "Buddy!!!" She turned out to be my friend's older sister, Lou. They lived less than half a block from my house in Sheboygan. I hadn't heard my nickname for over a year, so you can imagine my surprise. After the shock wore off, I told Lou what I wanted and she called her boss to come meet her neighbor from Sheboygan. The captain was very nice and explained to

The *Hope*, like its sister ships *Comfort* and *Mercy*, were decommissioned from the Navy and transferred to the Army. They were sailed by civilians in the Army Transport Service. The Army provided the medical service personnel.

me how I could be relieved from my present assignment and how he would get me onto the U.S.A.T. Hope, an Army Hospital ship.

As instructed, I went back to my post, went on sick call and was seen by an Army physician who was very irritated at having been recalled to serve once again. My plea was answered. A diagnosis was created. I now had Aironitis, which would be greatly relieved if I could serve on or near the sea. In less than 48 hours, I began my new assignment and boarded the Hope.

Once again, luck was running with me. They were painting the Army Complements Quarters on the ship, so I was temporarily assigned to a small ward shared with the First Sergeant. It took me two days to convince my roommate that I would be a real asset if I were assigned to the pharmacy. My strategy was to wake him at reveille begging to be assigned there. My good night whimper was the same. I got my wish but had to promise to shut up and not mention it again. Not hard to do when you get what you want. Nothing can happen unless you try.

Discretion Is Important

My assignment to the pharmacy on the hospital ship Hope was a wonderful break. I had decided to become a pharmacist and to begin college as soon as my tour of duty ended. To add to the blessing, my tutor had one more trip before he left the service, which would put me in charge of the pharmacy for the rest of my tour. I was a dedicated student and digested every word from my mentor. Maybe one too many.

I had the option of requesting things like bottled cough medicine. Or, if I preferred, I could get the active ingredients and make my own preparations. That appealed to me.

Since many products are ethyl-alcohol based, requisitions for gallons of the stuff were not questioned. Medical grade alcohol is about 190-proof, or 95 per cent pure. A premium bottled bourbon is 80 to 100 proof, or about 40 to 50 per cent alcohol.

After I took over, my first requisition from the supply depot included four gallons of ethyl alcohol. It went directly into locked storage. But, certain key people were aware of its presence and began negotiating with me for some. My most attractive offer came from the ship's electricians. I could have a refrigerator of my own. The only other person who had a refrigerator of his own was the captain of the ship. Plus, it would be kept full of ice cream.

All went well for a few days. One morning I was awakened abruptly with the shout, "Bring me my sextant, bring me my sextant!" The shout came from the bridge above. My quarters were located directly below the bridge.

Hawaii was in clear view, but we were not going to Hawaii. We were 600 miles off course! Ship captains do not take errors of this size too gracefully. Why were we so far off? It seems the gyro compasses were frozen in place. It seems their fluid is to be watched and added to daily, a responsibility of the ship's electricians, who happened to be drunk for several days and failed to check.

When I heard the story, I came close to panicking. Who would be the logical purveyor of the alcohol they consumed? I kept a very low profile. When we returned to San Francisco, the captain threw the electricians' bags onto the dock before the boarding ramp was even in place. They obviously were fired from their jobs, but to my knowledge, their supplier was never sought. That was the longest trip of my tour!

It's a Small World

I was standing next to the gangway of the hospital ship, observing our passengers board when I heard a yell, "Buddy!" A lovely lady charged at me with open arms. After my surprise hug, I asked her who she was. Her reply: "I was your baby-sitter, don't you recognize me?" As a government employee, she was on her way to Japan to provide administrative skills for our military occupation.

Almost a Statistic

Sometimes your mind blocks out scary incidents in your life, until one day, a reminder brings it all back.

I owned a pharmacy and decided that a Dale Carnegie course would give me the confidence to speak to groups and help develop my business. Upon completion of the course, I decided to work toward being a part-time lecturer with the firm. The first step in the process was to serve as a non-paid assistant to one of their lecturers. My function was to present examples on the spur of the moment on command. The lecturer would call out a topic and I had to run to the head of the class and make a coherent presentation of three to five minutes in length.

In one such session, he shouted, "Grube–fear!" It came back to me, the incident that occurred when I was a pharmacy technician on the Army hospital ship Hope.

One morning about 2 a.m., I was unable to sleep. I had always wanted to see the stars that formed the Southern Cross which is visible only from the South Pacific Ocean. I went to the boat deck where the life boats are mounted. The railing in that area consisted of three heavy cables instead of a waist-high metal wall. The spot I picked was close to the fantail, the stern of the ship where, below, the propellers drove the ship.

I sat on the top cable and hooked my toes into the lower cable and became enthralled with the beauty of the Southern Cross. I dozed off and did a back flip catching my fingers on the gunnel, or the narrow strip running around the ship. Mustering all the possible strength I could muster, I pulled myself up into the deck, and slithered across the deck on my stomach until I was inside the weather door. I arose, sweating profusely, and stopped and thanked God for saving me, for without His help, I would have been pulled into the propellers and chopped to shreds. Or, I could have been dumped into the Pacific Ocean thousands of miles from land. It could have been four hours or more before I'd even be missed.

As I write this 55 years later, I have tears in my eyes and fear in my heart. Many times since that talk, I have sat up in bed recalling that very night so long ago and being grateful to God for saving me.

My Service Was Ending

One of the ports of call for the Hope was Inchon, Korea. The harbor was not deep enough for the ship to dock, so it had to remain in the deeper water in the harbor. People and cargo were ferried from the ship to the dock by LCMs, small landing craft.

I decided to go ashore and look up a neighborhood friend, Jim Fassbender, who served in a Korean motor pool. Lacking confidence, I asked a shipmate to join me in finding Jim who suggested we meet at the Non-Commissioned Officers Club.

We easily found Jim. He was glad to see me and welcomed my friend, and the drinks flowed. Jim and I talked between sips of our beverages, but my friend drank consistently. The hours slipped by and when we headed for the dock, it became apparent that my friend was bombed. His staggering slowed us down and we missed the 10 o'clock LCM and had to wait 30 minutes for the next LCM to our ship.

The wait allowed my friend to pass out completely and revival was an unrealistic goal. He was a limp lump of GI. To get him on the LCM, I decided to pass him to someone already on board. So I placed one foot on the LCM and one on the dock and started to pass him to another. As I did, the vessel moved from the dock, putting me in a split position. The effect was devastating.

I succeeded in getting him on the LCM, but the next challenge was even worse. To get him on the ship, I had to carry him up a rope ladder. I succeeded, but again I put more strain on my body and a price would have to be paid.

In the morning, I went on sick call. I had ruptured myself and the doctor decided elective surgery was unwise at sea. I would be transferred to Letterman General Hospital in San Francisco for the operation.

Much to my chagrin, my hospital ship career was over. I wouldn't have enough time left on my tour of duty to make the complete circuit again. After surgery, a 30-day convalescent leave was in the offing. Sixty days of another assignment would follow before my tour of duty would end.

My last two months were spent in a medical distribution center supplying Army units in our area with medical supplies. It was a valuable experience that I used many times during my ensuing career.

More Military Service

Because I didn't want to lose the sergeant stripes I had earned during my first tour of duty, I had joined the army reserves. This gave me the opportunity to serve my country a second time. Thanks to ROTC accepting my two years of active duty, I was permitted to enroll in the reserves in my junior year in college and complete my education. I would then be commissioned a second lieutenant. I then found myself in the Korean War.

Vi Doki Hava Yes

Imagine yourself a second lieutenant in the medical service corps on your first assignment to a combat aid station. As you open the tent flaps, your first view is a huge sign. Listed across the top of the sign are twelve known venereal diseases and from top to bottom on the side, a list of Korean women's names from the area.

The bold check marks after the woman's name indicated which venereal disease she had. Some had all twelve, but they all had gonorrhea. It didn't take any imagination to recognize how serious this problem was. My sense was this was an epidemic that was difficult to control. Fidelity should have been every married GI's personal pledge, and total abstinence should have been the rule. Having sailed on the hospital ship Hope as an enlisted man five years earlier, I can attest to a large number of GI's who did not abstain.

Unfortunately, some of the diseases did not respond to the established treatments, creating a very difficult situation. This caused a great deal of concern to all medical personnel involved.

Fornication Control Left Something To Be Desired

With venereal diseases getting out of control, the battalion commander ordered all units to search and apprehend American GI's who were having intercourse with the Korean women. This became an additional duty of mine, to select dependable ranked enlisted men and assign them to a predesignated area on the dates selected for the search.

There were no manuals to refer to, no guidelines had been established. All the instructions we had was if you see GI's so occupied, stop them and order them to return to their tents.

I selected the two highest ranking sergeants in our aid station, provided them with powerful flashlights, and sent them on their way. Both men were physically big men, tall, powerfully built, and they were both very good soldiers. Their report at the end of the evening has stuck in my memory for these many years.

As they walked around each abode, flashlights glaring, they were unable to find anyone engaged until they saw a dimly-lighted shack. They decided to sneak up to find a couple at high fervor. One of the sergeants opened the door, picked up the male by the neck and his buttocks, and removed him from this shelter. His partner shone his light on the man's face and discovered he was a Korean. The sergeant carried him back in the same position and put him on top of his startled partner, who hadn't moved since the interruption!

After I stopped laughing I wondered if this incident could reflect on my orders. Fortunately, a few days later the major rescinded the order.

One's Appetite Can Be Spoiled

With gonorrhea so prevalent in Korea, I should have assumed that the lowest ranking medical officer in our medical platoon would be assigned to inspect every member of the battalion, one company at a time.

Our platoon leader was a captain; I was a second lieutenant. Guess who found himself with 300 men, penises in hand, examining each for heavy white excretions. If any appeared, the soldier was ordered to go to the MASH hospital for a test to confirm his gonorrhea. If the soldier failed to follow the instructions, and failed to put enough effort into the process, he had to repeat the performance for my edification.

My back was stiff from the frequent bending and my stomach was queasy, because all of the men were not careful about their hygiene.

We started our day at 5 a.m. One morning when I got to breakfast, the mess sergeant put two hard boiled eggs with a sausage the size of a bratwurst between them. I just wasn't hungry.

A Moonlight Requisition Saved Me Many, Dollars

The cease-fire accord that was signed at Panmunjon made it possible to reduce our forces in South Korea. We were told we could volunteer to leave the service. My plea was heard and accepted and so I was selected to return to the U.S. and leave the military.

That was wonderful news, until I discovered that I was personally signed for all the equipment in our aid station. A quick check of the list indicated I was short many thousands of dollars worth of equipment. I talked to my first sergeant about my dilemma. He said he was aware of the shortages and would take care of it.

When I asked, "How can you do that?" he said, "We will do a moonlight requisition, so don't worry, it will be here."

When the list was checked the next morning, I had plenty of equipment and I was able to sign off and leave without any complications.

The sergeant shared with me that they stole stuff from another medical platoon, and that very night they stole it back. People seemed to instinctively know how to work the system.

Saying Farewell

A common phrase in the military when you're leaving the service is "you stack arms." Usually four rifles are linked together when you stack arms.

Being a medic, stacking arms did not seem appropriate. So I stacked needles and placed them in front of the battalion commander's plate at breakfast. I formed a stack of four syringes and attached a brief note:

"Lt. Grube is stacking needles to commemorate leaving the battalion. I have great respect for the officers I was privileged to serve with, and will remember with pride that I was very lucky to serve with the very best."

–Al

Ken Benson's Family

The Wedding

Sally and I were all set to be married on June 23, 1951, in Plymouth, Wisconsin. The invitations had all been sent, St. Paul's Episcopal Church had been reserved, and the priest was ready to conduct the ceremony. But I almost didn't make it to the wedding!

I was stationed at Ft. Riley, Kansas. Several months before the wedding, Captain Labadie, of the 1st Radio Broadcasting and Leaflet Group, had assured me that I would have no problem in obtaining a two-week wedding furlough the last two weeks in June.

First Radio Broadcasting and Leaflet Group had been alerted for overseas duty; the Inspector General inspection was held just a few days before I was to depart via train for Wisconsin. Unfortunately, 1st Radio failed this critical inspection. All furloughs were canceled! I was in a panic.

The engagement photo of Alice (Sally) Drewry. At the time, she was a senior in art education at the University of Wisconsin-Madison. Ken had just graduated from the university and was serving in the Army.

I talked to Captain Labadie and he said there was nothing he could do. I talked to my good friends, George Menkart and Lee Nelson; they decided to assist me in organizing a campaign to persuade Wisconsin Senator Joe McCarthy that Private Benson should proceed to his wedding, notwithstanding the Inspector General's edict. I was also prepared to go A.W.O.L. if nothing else worked.

Fortunately, we didn't have to do either. Captain Labadie talked to 1st Radio's Commanding Officer, Colonel Homer Shields, about my dilemma. Colonel Shields made a personal visit to the Post Commanding General of Ft. Riley requesting that a special exception be made for Private Benson and that he be authorized to immediately take leave for his wedding. The Commanding General authorized the exception provided Pvt. Benson leave all government property at Ft. Riley upon his departure. Lt. Schall drove me to the train depot in Junction City, Kansas. I was wearing a glen-plaid suit, carried no uniforms or any other government property and boarded the train for Wisconsin posed as civilian.

The newlyweds greet their parents. From left, Carl and Ottilia Benson, Sally, Ken, Carol and Charles Drewry.

A Journey in the Ark,

by Dick Lemmerhirt, in the Kohler Co. newsletter, "People," July, 1971.

In the summer of 1971, Ken Benson and 15 relatives took an 18-day trip from Sheboygan to Oregon and back in a converted school bus. The travelers included Ken's wife, Sally; their five children; Sally's brother, Hugh Drewry, his wife and their nine children. They visited Sally's sister and her family in Vale, Oregon.

The bus, a 1961 Wayne 54-passenger school bus, was purchased in 1970 at the Sheboygan County Fair. It was stripped of its seats and then equipped with beds, a kitchen, a toilet and new seats and tables. "We figured we got a real bargain, even though we spent most of the winter renovating it," Ken said.

On the journey, ten people slept in the bus, named "The Ark," and six slept in a tent. They took their time, stopping to fish and see the sights along the way. They survived a severe thunderstorm in Iowa, blowing snow as they crossed through Rocky Mountain National Park at 12,600 feet, and two minor breakdowns. Not once during the journey did the travelers enjoy a restaurant meal or a motel bed. Instead, the wives cooked hearty breakfasts before beginning the day's journey, ate sandwiches prepared by the girls for lunch, and cooked dinners of lasagna, Swedish meatballs, trout, ham, and steak.

"You may not believe it," Ken said, "but a long trip with 16 people in a big bus is less frazzling than a trip in a station wagon with five kids. I'd have no hesitation about doing it again."

The Ark and its passengers, from left, are Hugh Drewry, Ken Benson (in bus), Sally Benson, Mrs. Drewry, Andy Drewry, Jennifer Benson, Jim Drewry, Liz and Ken Benson, Matthew and Mary Drewry, Nate Benson, Phillip Drewry, Jon Benson and Julie and Paul Drewry. Brownie, the Benson's dog, did not join the travelers.

Trick or Treat

It was a sunny, Sunday afternoon on October 31, 1971. Sally and I and four of our five children, Liz, Ken, Jon and Nate, drove out to our old mill house on the Onion River in Winooski, Town of Lyndon, Sheboygan County. A few hours earlier, at our home in Sheboygan, we had waved good-bye to our oldest daughter, sixteen-year-old Jennifer and her Girl Scout friends Debbie Tompsett and Mary Jo Stetson. The three of them were driving out to the Kettle Moraine area to participate in a Boy Scout Safe Driving Rally. Debbie was behind the wheel, Mary Jo was in the front seat and Jennifer sat in the back seat. The girls were all members of Sally's Girl Scout Troop. They were in good spirits as Debbie drove away.

Sally and I and the kids were getting things picked up, cleaned up and freshened up at the mill house before winter set in. Sally and the kids were in the vegetable garden picking up some cabbage and pumpkins and I began mowing the lawn. The trees were in full autumn color; the grass needed one last mowing. I was grumpy because I couldn't get the mower started. There was a lot of grass to mow before we could return home to Sheboygan. Finally, I got the mower started, finishing the job much later than I expected. As the sun was setting, we all piled into the station wagon for the sixteen-mile return trip to the comforts of our home in Sheboygan. My grumpiness persisted as I wearily drove home, knowing that my inoperable mower had deprived me of precious reading time of my Sunday paper.

It was sometime after 7:00 p.m. before we had all settled down.

The phone rang; it was Sarah, a girl-scout friend of Jennifer's.

"Mr. Benson, is Jenny home yet?"

"No," I replied, "Why do you ask?"

"I was concerned," Sarah said. "I heard that there was a terrible traffic accident this afternoon and I wanted to know if Jenny is OK."

That phone conversation changed our lives. I called the Sheboygan Police Department. They informed me that there indeed had been a tragic truck-auto collision on Highway 57 at the intersection of Woodlawn Road. There were three passengers in the car and one driver in the truck. The truck driver survived; but there were two fatalities in the car; Art Tompsett had identified his daughter, Debbie, as one of the deceased. The other body had been transported to the Sheboygan County Morgue; the third survivor had been transported by ambulance from the Plymouth Hospital to St. Joseph Hospital in Milwaukee as an "unidentified female, about twenty-one years old."

I drove to the Sheboygan Police station. The officer on duty directed me to the morgue in the basement of the courthouse. As I approached the dark entrance I saw Dallas Stetson also making his way to the doorway. A deputy sheriff unlocked the door. Dallas and I entered the small, windowless room. We stood motionless next to the sheet-covered body on the stretcher; the officer gently lifted the sheet from the upper body. Dallas collapsed in my arms. It was his daughter, Mary Jo. I hurried home. Sally and I gathered our children in a close circle of prayer in our parlor; we put our arms around each other and prayed for Jenny. We called Millie Acker, a nearby neighbor, to baby-sit. We explained to the children that Sally and I were about to drive to the intensive care ward at St. Joseph Hospital to find Jenny and talk to her doctor.

The sixty-mile drive to Milwaukee seemed endless.

We met Dr. Berglund, a neurosurgeon, in the waiting room outside the intensive care unit. He explained that Jenny was comatose. He had administered blood thinner as soon as she arrived from Plymouth. He said that Jenny had sustained severe brain damage from the collision. Her brain had

The Benson family, December 31, 1967. Front: Jon and Nate. Middle: Jennifer, Liz, and Sally. Back: Kenner and Ken.

been badly bruised within her skull. She had a contusion on her left eye and was comatose. There were no broken bones. Dr. Berglund could not offer much hope. Jennifer was experiencing Cheyne-Stokes respiration, a pattern of thirty or forty seconds between each breath; she was severely injured. Dr. Berglund told us that the longer Jenny remained unconscious the less likely she would be normal or even survive.

The Electric Typewriter

Christmas 1971 was approaching. On December 6, Jennifer was transferred from St. Joseph's Hospital in Milwaukee to Memorial Hospital in Sheboygan. She remained comatose and had shown little improvement since her October 31 accident.

Miss Olson, the managing director of Memorial Hospital, showed little interest in admitting Jennifer as a patient. She suggested that it might be better to place Jenny in a nursing home. She expressed doubts as to whether or not her staff could fulfill Jenny's needs. I finally agreed that Sally and I would provide independent evening care, at our expense, if the hospital would admit her. Miss Olson agreed to this proposal. Sally and I eventually had as many as sixteen part-time workers on our payroll.

It was apparent that Miss Olson and her staff believed that our beautiful sixteen-year old daughter was destined to remain a "vegetable" for life. In other words, if we faced reality, a nursing home would be the best placement for Jenny in her condition.

The days passed without progress. Dr. James Michael made his daily rounds. Mary Doll visited the hospital daily cheerfully chatting; she sang to Jenny, hopefully reminding her of the wonderful Sheboygan Community Players musicals in which Mary had performed. Our dear friend Lu French was a daily visitor, gently and prayerfully supporting Jenny in her comatose state.

Mary Wilke, whose daughter Sharon was in Jenny's scout troop, presented Jenny with a whirling Santa Claus musical toy that played "Jingle Bells". Sally and I spent countless hours talking with Jenny even though she didn't respond. Claire and Irene were key players. They were staff nurse assistants; they breathed hope and life into Jenny's daily routine through their tender love and care.

Sally was concerned about the condition of Jennifer's feet and hands. She didn't want them to atrophy from lack of use. She would religiously massage them several times a day to avoid dropped feet or dysfunctional hands.

We played cassettes; we placed earphones over Jenny's head, playing her favorite songs over and over as time passed by. Friends would visit Jenny's room; our children were given the opportunity to see her.

Our friends overwhelmed us with their loving support. Meals arrived at our home for the family on a regular basis. Flowers and cuddly toys filled Jennifer's room to overflowing. Sally remained at Jenny's bedside through most of each day.

One afternoon, I walked out of Jenny's room in despair. I decided to buy Jenny her Christmas present. I just couldn't bring myself to buy another stuffed animal. Instead I bought Jenny an electric typewriter! It was Christmas Eve; I placed the typewriter next to Jenny's bed and wished her a Merry Christmas.

By the summer of 1972, Jenny began typing lessons at Plymouth High School.

Square Root

February 26, 1972 -- At the urging of friends, Sally and I took a Saturday evening off from hospital duty and attended the Sheboygan County Medical Society Ball at the Executive Inn. Dining and ballroom dancing was a pleasant relief compared to the past four months of tending to Jennifer's hospital room needs.

That very evening, in our absence, Jennifer spoke her first words to Claire. She mumbled "mother, father, sister, brother." Then she mumbled the names of the attending nurse and nurse assistants. She was apparently reading the name tags! We were delighted to hear the good news.

On the following Monday afternoon, Jenny's close friend Beth DeVrys visited her. Beth would say "dog" and Jenny would slowly say "Brownie", which was the name of her dog. Beth and Jenny tried unsuccessfully to engage in conversation; it was just too painful and slow going and extremely fatiguing for Jenny as well.

Beth then asked Sally if there was something else they might do that would be less fatiguing and more stimulating for Jennifer. Sally suggested that they work on simple arithmetic problems, with Jennifer holding up her fingers in answer to the problems rather than verbalizing the numbers.

Beth started with simple addition, "two plus two?" After a contemplative pause, four fingers unfolded from Jenny's clenched fist. "Three plus three?" Six fingers were held out. "Three times three?" Nine fingers. "The square root of nine plus the square root of twenty-five?" Jenny was a little slower on this one; after a long, silent, pause she held out eight fingers. She had correctly computed the sum of the square root of two numbers in her head and digitally displayed her answer to Beth.

That evening when Dr. Michael was making his rounds I related Jennifer's mathematical accomplishment to him. He was astounded.

Family

Sally's parents, Carol and Charles Drewry lived on a farm in Winooski, sixteen miles west of Sheboygan. On February 9, 1967, they were both killed in an auto accident in Florida.

Prior to their death, Sally and I and all of our children spent many wonderful hours with Carol and Charlie visiting the farm. They were good grandparents. Three of Sally's brothers eventually all lived in Winooski so the family has remained close to us. Our children have been blessed with an abundance of cousins, aunts and uncles.

We are a close family. Jennifer's auto accident on October 31, 1971 changed our lives. We love and are proud of each and every one of our children. We are especially thankful of all of their support in helping us to permit Jennifer to reach her optimal level of independence.

Sally

Sally is my best friend, lover and wife. We have been married more than fifty-five years. Two weeks after our wedding on June 23, 1951, I was shipped overseas; it was sixteen long months of separation before Sally arrived in Tokyo on October 13, 1952.

We are a peripatetic couple.

We have traveled, hiked, sailed, canoed, motored, biked, trained, camped and flown. We visited Scandinavia with

A family portrait from Christmas, 1978. Front row: Ken, Liz, Jennifer and Luke, her dog. Back row: Sally, Ken and Nate. Jon's picture is on the mantle. He was an AFS exchange student in New Zealand at the time.

our family and my parents. We visited China twice. We have viewed both the extreme east and west of the Great Wall of China. We traveled by rail from Beijing, across the Gobi Desert and on to Kazakhstan, Uzbekistan, up the shores of the Caspian Sea to Moscow and flew on to St. Petersburg. We hiked the jungles of Uganda, including a one-hour visit with a family of thirteen gorillas. We Land Rovered among the acacia trees and hot air ballooned over the Serengeti in Kenya, viewing first hand the animal life of Africa. We bicycled across Burgundy, Normandy and along the Dordogne River in France. We strolled down the streets of Paris, Florence, and Rome.

We hiked the trails in the Alps. We boated with our son Nate and Joelle into the remote jungles of the Brazilian Pantenole International Bird Sanctuary near the Bolivian border. We motored about the North and South Islands of New Zealand and western Australia with our son Jon and Crystal. We visited our daughter Liz in London while she attended Goldsmith College. Among our many visits to London, we also toured both London and Sweden with our son Nate and his wife Jessica. We hiked the Lake District with our friends Sandy and George Kunkle. We canoed the Boundary Waters of Minnesota and Quetico, Canada with our son Jon and Crystal. We toured Alaska with our grandson Ben. We enjoyed Washington D.C.

with our grandson, Carl. We took the train from Minneapolis to Glacier National Park, Montana with our son Ken, his wife LaVonne and Carl. We experienced the 1996 Atlanta Olympics with the Forer families and Carl. We biked across Death Valley, camping in the desert. We have touched base in all fifty states during our lifetime.

We raised five wonderful children–Jennifer, Liz, Ken, Jon and Nate– to adulthood, experiencing all the challenges, joys, trials, tribulations and miracles of family.

Sally is both creative and proactive. She visualizes things in three dimensions; tasteful, artistic and sometimes unorthodox ideas rapidly spring from her mind. Sally gets things done. Sometimes she does not express herself clearly, but if I listen carefully to her, I am often able to both articulate and write about her creative concepts, thus enabling her to successfully accomplish the tasks she envisions. As a team we successfully contributed our mutual skills toward building the St. Francis by the Sea Episcopal Church at Salter Path, N.C. Building the church required the dedicated work of the entire congregation. Sally worked almost full time for three years as chairperson of the architectural and building committee; she was the designated contract representative for St. Francis Episcopal Church, serving as liaison between the architect, contractor and vestry. The church was built within budget, plus extras that cost less than ten per cent more than the original contract price. The vestry recognized Sally's leadership.

Sally is a creative mother, homemaker, cook, commercial artist, landscaper, gardener, floral designer, caregiver, animal trainer and seamstress. Were it not for her persistence, Jennifer would have been salted away in a nursing home thirty-six years ago. It was Sally who intervened when drugs were unwisely administered to stop Jennifer from repetitive sit-ups and body movements. Instead, Sally and YMCA director Don Lohman hauled gym

May 1, 2004, on Sally's 75th birthday.

mats up to Jennifer's hospital room, placed them wall to wall on the floor and let her flail about until she began her long, hard struggle back to consciousness.

Sally and I complement each other by our differences. We often disagree; then, we try to work it out together. The quality of our joint decisions has been enhanced by the reconciliation of our differences. We manage to broaden our horizons when we truly listen to each other.

Sally is creative and visionary. I am articulate, realistic and practical. I would have missed some of the best ideas and experiences of my life were it not for Sally. She has kept me from being boring.

We are in love. We try to listen. We are candid. We have total trust. We never lie to each other. We reconcile our differences when they seem irreconcilable. It is our deep love that sustains us.

Ken and Sally cross-country ski in Yellow-stone National Park.

Sally and Ken on her sailboat off Pine Knoll Shores, North Carolina.

A Dog's Life

by Ken Benson. Written for the Vollrath Company newsletter, V.I.P.

It is noon on March 3, 1987, in Chico Hot Springs, Montana. Our luggage is packed. Sally and I have two hours before the bus leaves for the airport in Bozeman for our flight to Milwaukee. An awesome and vigorous one-week vacation of cross-country skiing in Yellowstone National Park is over. The Riveredge-sponsored outing has permitted us to enjoy the very best of nature and to meet new friends.

We decided to join Peg, Carol and Ilse for a short hike up a barren steep hill at the base of the snow-covered mountains. Fifty degrees, no snow, an easy climb up the hillside toward a small lake that Carol discovered on an earlier hike with Dick.

Two frolicking golden retrievers join us from the hotel. Kona and her seven month old daughter, Tootsie.

Other hikers from our group join us as they come down the hill to return to the bus. Kona and Tootsie romp toward the center of the pond. They break through the ice and are immersed in a cold water trap. They try to get footing on the edges of the icy water hole, but slip back into the cold water. Each attempt to escape becomes more frantic. Kona gets her font paws on the edge of the ice and painfully pulls her back legs closer to the edge as her front legs slither forward.

We call and coax the dogs to come to shore. We tensely gather at the edge of the pond knowing that death is imminent. Kona responds to our calls and valiantly gathers that last ounce of strength that pulls her over the ice. Then she gingerly and cautiously runs across the ice to the shore. She looks at us as if begging us to save her daughter.

There are now twelve of us. Arnie, Judy, Jim, Carol, Bob, Nan and

Tootsie tries to stay afloat in the freezing water as Arnie pushes a branch toward the hole in the ice. Ken Benson, knee-deep in water, hangs on to Arnie's belt.

Ann have joined us from the hillside. We gather our resources as we watch Tootsie thrash about in panic in the water trap. She goes under. Her head bobs back through the water and she emits a mournful howl. But in all her thrashing and with all our coaxing, she is unable to free herself.

Twelve people on a first-name basis are bonded together in a mission: Save Tootsie without giving our lives. Random thoughts–take off our belts, link them together–no, it won't work, Tootsie is more than 50 feet from the shore. Stretch out on the ice in a human chain to help the pup get footing– no, too risky, the ice is thin and we don't know how deep the water is.

Arnie is our leader. He is willing to take greater risk to save Tootsie. He goes to the shore and cautiously starts to test the ice, but breaks through. Judy warns him not to go out. Arnie comes back and we look for a large tree limb. Jim finds one. It is heavy and more than 25 feet long. We all carry it to shore.

Arnie is at the front and cautiously breaks through the ice up to his waist as I hold on to the waist of his trousers and break through the ice over my boot tops. Ann is behind me. We stop. We all agree to try to thrust the limb across the ice to the water hole.

Everyone gathers strength to push the limb across the ice. Now! But the limb only slides near the edge of the hole, not far enough to help Tootsie. Depressed silence. We then take a long branch and try to push the limp further toward the water hole. We collectively strain to push the big limb slowly towards Tootsie. The limb moves to the edge of the water hole. We call Tootsie, but in her panic, she doesn't understand. Her strength is ebbing.

The end of the limb at the water hole is forked and a branch angles out from the limb about a foot above the edge of the ice. Tootsie manages to briefly thrust her front paws on the limb, but quickly lets go and turns away in panic from our wooden lifeline.

We all run to position ourselves to her hind side. Tootsie turns toward the limb in response to our calls. She sticks her shoulders under the forked branch and pushes against it. The downward force enables her to push her rear paws against the ice. She slowly and tenuously slithers out of the water hole. We cheer! Tootsie gingerly walks over the ice to shore.

Her concerned mom greets her. Tootsie shakes cold water on her lifesavers and continues her romp down the hill with mom. Mission accomplished! A close bond envelops a team on its way downhill to catch a bus home.

The May 27, 1990, wedding of the Benson's youngest son, Nate, to Jessica Oakes. From left: Mel Oakes, Sally Benson, Nate, Jessica, Penny Oakes, Ken Benson.

The Benson family at daughter Elizabeth's wedding on June 18, 1983

Ken and Sally Benson's Seven Grandsons

Carl, Nathaniel and Benjamin

Isaac

Alex

Ken, Jon, Dylan on Sally's sailboat in North Carolina.

Elijah

Ken and LaVonne's wedding, April 8, 1989. From left: Ken, Jennifer, Sally, Jon, Crystal, Nate, LaVonne, Ken, Liz, Ben, Dan.

Al Grube's Family

I loved my own family and was fortunate to have two loving daughters who make me very proud of their successes.

Although my first marriage to Marjory ended in divorce, there were many fun and productive periods in our 29 years together.

Fortunately, after our separation, I found the love of my life, and so far I have enjoyed 25 wonderful years with Mary. I am looking forward to many more years together.

The love of my life, Mary.

Marjory

In 1952, during the second semester of my senior year at the University of Wisconsin, I met a gal who knew how to sing songs and tell interesting stories. The only way I could learn the songs and stories was to date Marjory Panetti and have her teach them to me. So date her I did.

We finished the semester and she decided to remain in Madison for the summer session while I waited for my call to enter the service. Toward the end of August, I bid her farewell with the suggestion that if I received a state-side assignment we would consider marriage. If I was sent directly to Korea I would not consider it, since the Korean War was raging at that point and the Americans and their South Korean allies had been pushed almost all the way south to Pusan River and faced a bleak future.

As it happened, I received a state-side assignment and a 14-day leave to return to Madison and to my future bride.

It was mid-October and we went out-of-state to tie the knot. As newly-weds we moved all about. Almost a year elapsed before the dreaded Korean assignment came along. During the interim, we had purchased a house trailer which we pulled to Madison. Marjory returned to school and I was off to Korea in 1953.

American forces and their South Korean allies had succeeded in pushing the North Koreans all the way to Panmunjon, about in the middle of the country, where they fought to a stalemate. Ultimately, a cease-fire was arranged and combat stopped.

In the passion of the moment, on our last evening together before I shipped off to Korea, Marjory became impregnated with our first daughter,

Lauren Amanda. Later when the news was confirmed, I became eager to return to the states.

Lisa, Everyone's Friend

Our second daughter, Lisa Ruth, was a collector of friends and admirers. She was always involved in some fun project, but school was not in that category. One evening she was bogged down in school work and was having a very difficult time doing her homework.

Since her father wasn't an academic, her mother was the logical choice for assistance. In fact, Marjory was an "A" student in college. She possessed an almost photographic memory and always impressed everyone with her ability to learn, digest, and retain anything she set her mind to.

Lisa said she did not understand her assignment, much less how to do the homework. So Marjory volunteered to assist her. Marjory put her whole self into the project, as Lisa watched and listened. A bit later, I ran into Lisa leaving and assumed she and Marjory had finished. About 30 minutes later I walked into the kitchen, where they had been working. Marjory looked up and asked where Lisa was. My answer, of course, was she left the house 30 minutes earlier. Her homework was completed, but not by her.

A Lesson in Economics

Lauren was approaching college graduation when she announced she was going to marry her college sweetheart, a nice young man from a small community near Sheboygan.

During the opening discussion she announced that she would prefer her guests be family, friends, and relatives; not associates from the store or customers. I wasn't pleased to hear that, but I decided to accept her wishes at that moment in time.

Later, Lauren announced that she was anticipating 700 guests. It was then that I pointed out to her that if we had more than 350 guests we would have to include Grube Pharmacy staff and our better customers.

Her reply was, "Oh, we only will have about 150. The groom has a big family and many closer friends." At that point, I lost my cool and went into orbit. I was furious, and said lots of things I am not proud of to this very day.

Fortunately, Marjory realized this was too serious to let pass, but required a complete change of direction. The cost of wedding Lauren wanted was at least $10,000. In the early 1960's, that was a lot of money.

Marjory's proposal was that we would give them the $10,000 and they could pay for the event. If it cost more, they must cover it. If less, they could use it as they saw fit. The wedding had 25 guests and was held at a friend's home. They honeymooned in the Bahamas and had some money left over for household furnishings.

Thanks, Marjory.

Lisa, Al and Lauren.

Al and Lisa. It is always special to have your children come home.

Al and Lauren. Some very special gifts for me.

Community Theater

Community Theater became a bigger and bigger part of Marjory's life. I became a little jealous of time she spent with the theater and felt I needed to take action. My own work schedule was down to less than 50 hours a week and I had the time and money to pursue outside interests of my own. I don't remember which of my family members suggested it, but the essence was "It is always easier to destroy an activity from the inside."

So I became active in Community Theater, my first effort was to become friends with the director. Not too difficult a task because I respected him and did like him. Dave Bryant, the director, wasn't sold on my talent but he felt my personality would click with an audience. He thought that if he stuck with parts that were 15 per cent of either side of my personality, I could pull it off.

To reduce any economic loss I might suffer if I had to replace myself at the drugstore, I was awarded third-act parts. I was pleasantly surprised at how many fun roles only appeared

Tony Larson and Al Grube doing song and dance in *Kiss Me Kate.* Though not the leads, they did have a personal curtain call.

in the third act, and fit me personally very well. I appeared in quite a few roles over the years, and enjoyed every one and became enamored with the stage.

Marjory's personal desire was to be on the board of directors of the Community Theater. But when there was an opening on the board, several board members proposed Al Grube instead of Marjory. Apparently my business background made me a desirable addition. Can you imagine Marjory's annoyance when it was her husband who won the seat she had hoped to fill?

Acting Can Have Consequences

I grew to like participating in community theater. It was a pleasant break from the daily grind. I loved my job, but I needed to think about something else to reduce the pressure from time to time. The director, Dave Bryant, became a personal friend.

In "The Man Who Came to Dinner," I tried to be one of the Marx brothers. As I entered the scene for the first time, the maid was supposed to walk down the steps from the second floor and fall on my shoulder. She was heavier than I and I dropped her in the first rehearsal. She made a lot of noise, but no real damage occurred.

Upon my insistence, we changed the scene to my greeting her as she came off the steps. I would then do a dance step and throw her out and retrieve her. After several performances, my right arm was so stretched that I could scratch below my knee without bending. I was out of balance.

Two decades later, the chiropractor who adjusted my shoulder is still enjoying my story.

A Deterrent

For twenty-nine years, two daughters, and a real struggle to make the marriage work, Marjory hung in there. I sensed that once the girls left the nest, Marjory would be considering the same option. Once the corner had been turned, she wanted her own life.

She talked about taking a shot at being a professional actress. I was convinced that with her passion for community players and the many accolades she received after each performance, that one day she would give her dream a try.

She had also expressed an interest in running a card and gift shop. An ideal location became available next to the largest retailer in downtown Sheboygan, so I leased it. I assumed that she would identify with the business, run it without my input and stay in Sheboygan.

It did postpone her leaving for a few years. But ultimately, she made the decision with a half-hearted request that I could join her in her quest of a professional acting career.

Now that I had put in more than two decades in my business, and the rewards from it made my life comfortable, I did not view that offer as an option, and I did not accept it.

Life Changes

It wasn't long before Marjory decided to go to California and study with a teacher who built a reputation for helping talented actors become true professionals. So, in the summer of 1980, she was off. The children were gone from our home, either working or studying at UW-Madison.

I kept myself busy that summer, but my instincts told me that next summer I would be alone, a fact I refused to face. Although I didn't push the ladies away, neither did I solicit their attention.

With the fall, Marjory returned, but her interest in our home had waned and the card and gift store lost its appeal. Her approach to day-to-day life was she either dressed like a beauty contestant or a bag lady. I couldn't predict which it would be, and I found myself either proud of her appearance or trying to hide to avoid my embarrassment.

By January 1981, Marjory began to cry every hour I was present. The rumor had it she hoped to push me into a divorce, getting me to take the initiative. That way, the guilt would be mine instead of hers. I insisted that she must see a psychiatrist, which she did.

Marjory left me on Memorial Day and went to California. It took two attempts for her to leave. She had car problems just after leaving, returned, had the car fixed, and then left again for the last time. I was absolutely crushed. My marriage and my family were over. My life was in for a major change and I knew my own family would look upon this as a failure on my part.

I'm not a Casanova and thought it would be tough to date women once again. I discovered that was not to be a problem. It almost seemed that the ladies saw me as a good catch. I didn't feel undesirable at all.

Lucky Date

A friend of mine in another community introduced me to his female friend. Since he was married, I didn't realize that this lady was his girlfriend and I started to date her. I remember on our first date at the end of the evening she said, "I never go to bed on the first date. When would you like to go out again?"

It set me back as I actually did not have any plans like that, but I did ask her out again. She was true to her word, and it became apparent after a few dates that she was an interesting date, but not a potential mate. Then I discovered she was my buddy's extracurricular activity. Sensing that I was looking for something more lasting, she introduced me to her dear friend, Mary. It seemed to me that she had decided that Mary and I were similar types.

I was invited to attend a sales training program for potential franchisees. Mary was planning to attend and I could meet her without the obligation to take her out. The attraction was instantaneous and we began to chat. Eventually, Mary took me back to her home after going more than 20 miles in the wrong direction. Before we parted, we had plans for several dates in the next week, including her

My beautiful, fun-loving bride to be, Mary Lee.

birthday, my lucky day. My concern was I had eleven years on her. She was in her early 40's and I was in my 50's. Could I be too old for her?

Love of My Life

Mary turned out to be everything Marjory was not. She was small in stature, about five feet tall, as opposed to Marjory's 5'7" against my 5'8". She was pretty–my definition would be beautiful. She had an exciting build, very well-proportioned, and her appearance was perfection. Any man would be proud to have her as his mate. She was also very bright, practical, and reasonable.

Our attraction became love and a deep desire to be together. As the summer of 1982 ended, her home was sold and she needed to move. I wanted her to be mine and all mine forever. I convinced her to move to Sheboygan and live with me. I would ask Marjory for a divorce and once final, we would marry.

She had one child still at home and I offered to accept responsibility for Teresa. As she grew up, she became my third daughter. Her presence rounded out my life and gave me an opportunity to show my own children how much I cared for them.

I also acquired three grown sons as well. They didn't join us immediately, but two of the three shared a portion of their lives with me. Jon liked me from the start. He promoted me to his mother. Prior to the first Iraq war, Desert Storm, he spent several months with us as he waited to be called into service. Once Jon moved on, Dan, the eldest, moved in to go to nearby Lakeshore Technical College. He stayed for two years. He always seemed

The Rev. Reed Forbush, pastor of the First Congregational Church in Sheboygan, embraces Al and Mary after the wedding ceremony on February 14, 1983.

to be very bright, but he never could develop a direction. At age 45, he still hasn't found one. However, we continue to hope. Tom, the youngest son, has lots of mechanical skills, but lacks confidence in his own intelligence, putting himself down and allowing people to take advantage of him. I was unable to help them, which saddened me.

Once together, Mary proved to be the love of my life. She was a "neatnik" like my mother and I realized that was very important to me. I am organized and appreciated that characteristic. Her decor ideas matched my own. Avante garde was Marjory's approach and I was not really comfortable in my own surroundings. Now I fit in.

Whenever I appear in public, I know if I checked with Mary before I left home, people will comment on the fact that I look sharp. Even our politics match, and we enjoy the same TV programs and movies. One of our favorite things to do is to visit with one another. At events, we instinctively support one another, leaving the other only when we are sure our mate is comfortable and not straining to be part of the group.

There probably is no perfect relationship, but ours comes close enough for me. At this writing, we have enjoyed 25 years of martial bliss. God willing, it will go on for a long while yet. Each day we are together is a blessing to me.

Divorce is Costly

Marjory recommended that Mary and I just live together. She felt a divorce was unnecessary. Neither Mary nor I concurred with her evaluation. We wanted to make the commitment of marriage and be together until the end of our days. We prevailed and Marjory finally agreed.

I was prepared to give Marjory half of everything we had accumulated, but none of our holdings were liquid. In fact, cash was in very short supply. My offer was to have professionals representing neither side establish the net worth of our existing businesses. She could take any or all the businesses other than the drugstore.

Since she had moved to California, it would be awkward for her to manage or even sell her portion, so all of the negotiation was done in absentia and her attorney convinced the presiding judge that his client would accept a reasonable evaluation. I could make payments plus ten per cent interest on Marjory's half of our assets. This was at a time when typical interest rates were 3 to 4 per cent.

The judge ruled in Marjory's favor and it took us ten years to buy her half. Marjory did us one favor. She agreed to value our home at its original purchase price, even though by then it had appreciated. We live in that home today and love it.

Mary's decorating skills have made it the envy of many of our friends. It's funny how a childhood dream coming true can make the home even more special. We have an in-ground swimming pool and each day in the summer I swim laps. I remind myself that the swimming pool is a symbol that my working life was an economic success. The pool has been there 38 years.

Incidentally, Mary helped me to not only regain my net worth of 25 years earlier, but actually exceed it.

Additional Thoughts

Hopefully, the preceding stories of some of the incidents in my life gave you an overview of my life and in a small way helped you to understand why I am an advocate of the business principles we will share with you.

There are three additional thoughts I would like to share with you, because I believe that to a large degree they were an aid to my longevity and the interests I enjoy in my aging years.

1) Exercising daily keeps your body fit and permits you to enjoy your silver years because you are still able to do things.

2) Watching your weight and returning it to what it was when you were younger permits better health and flexibility of movement. Today Mary and I find half portions sufficient to satisfy our hunger and keep our weight at where we feel the best. Believe it or not, a half cookie is as enjoyable as a whole one.

3) Travel is fun, educational, and helps you to appreciate your homeland. It gives you a better understanding of the many advantages we enjoy and the dilemmas other people face.

I assume each of you have a religious belief and are grateful to your creator for life itself. To me this belief is essential to enjoy a rewarding life.

It is my belief that your priorities in life should be as follows:

1st: God

2nd: family

3rd: job

I feel that sequence is essential for true happiness.

Longevity is enhanced by love,
by happiness, and by discipline

1. *Mate*

2. *Occupation*

3. *Exercise*

4. *Meditation*

5. *Eating wisely*

6. *Supplements*

7. *Reading, studying, & learning*

8. *Volunteering*

9. *Friends and fun*

10. *Prayers of gratitude*

Al carries this card in his day plan-
ner. The sequence of importance must
be determined by each person on an
individual basis, but the ten areas are
worthy of consideration if longevity is
desired.

Our home looks small, but it is more than adequate.

Our swimming pool is proof that I enjoyed some success in my career. We all need that assurance from time to time.

Our youngest child, Teresa, and her husband, Troy, swim in our pool with their two children, Delaney and Ramsey.

Birthdays can be fun and memorable.

Al has a costume for the activities he enjoys, like biking.

Mary is not only pretty, but a wonderful partner. Her many efforts to make our life together special are really enjoyed.

Biking in Washington state. From left, Dawn and Don Bellau, Mary and Al Grube, Phyllis Zeiner. Dick Zeiner was our photographer.

Cross-country skiing was our favorite winter sport. Dawn and Don Bellau were always ready to go.

The Grube's took a three-week trip to China in 2003. They visited Shanghai, Beijing, the Great Wall and other sites. "The trip was wonderful," said Al. "We were very impressed with the country."

Mary and Al in the West- proof that we really did it.

Work: Al Grube

Long Wait

Opening businesses without capital puts a terrific strain on the entrepreneur and his mate. Lauren, our first daughter, was actually three years old before I saw her awake.

I left the house before 8 in the morning to prepare the store for 9 a.m. opening. I ate all my meals except breakfast on the run, closed the store at 9 p.m. and spent another hour with closing procedures. This routine was followed seven days a week with one day off every 28 days, a real full-time job. Working almost 100 hours a week became the norm. I did that for half of the salary I received for the nine months I worked at Walgreens before opening my own store.

It took almost three years before the store stopped losing money. It was no easy task, but in the end I did succeed, and we quickly slipped into the middle class. Moving from second floor double flats into our own home was a real thrill. It made us feel we had arrived.

All Suggestions Aren't Dumb

Being present in a nursing home as a pharmacist can be of value to the patients from time to time.

The Director of Nursing in the Morningside Nursing Home stopped at the pharmacy to share her concern about a ambulatory patient, who literally bounced off the walls as he tried to navigate the hallway from his room to the nursing station, hitting both sides of the walkway as he proceeded.

I suggested we review his chart and his meds to see if any of the medications could precipitate this behavior. It became obvious almost immediately. He was taking three potent diuretics to control his er-

When this photo was taken in the 1970s, Grube Drugs had grown to four pharmacists.

ratic blood pressure, but it also removed all the potassium from his system. Consequently, the erratic walking pattern.

My suggestion to the Director of Nursing was to contact the physician and ask if he might prescribe a potassium supplement.

When she asked the doctor, who became quite irritable, he demanded to know who offered this suggestion. The pharmacist, Al Grube, was her reply. He shouted, "Tell Grube if he wants to practice medicine, go to medical school!" Fortunately, three weeks later an order went through for the potassium and within 48 hours, our patient walked as straight as an arrow.

Thank heavens. Today this probably wouldn't happen.

Don't Underestimate the Ladies

Our pharmacy had a trash container built into the counter. The trash container was made of heavy material, much heavier than was needed for the task assigned to it–holding discarded paper and prescription bottles.

One day, Roger, our stock boy, came to empty the container which was stuffed with a full load of trash. He struggled to take it out and then put it on top of the counter to catch his breath.

Sam, one of the female clerks, came by and said, "Who left this here?" She lifted it off of the counter and set it aside with no effort at all!

Roger was embarrassed that such a small woman was stronger than he. The laughter was deafening. Roger never mentioned his weight-lifting classes again!

Tell That Hypochondriac!

Our prescription department ran along the left side of the pharmacy. A checkout station was in front of the prescription department, near the entrance.

The pharmacist phone was located close to the checkout area. The phone was attached to a recorder that also could serve as a speaker-phone. A long cord on the phone allowed the pharmacist reach any area in the department to look for a medication or find additional information from the package insert included with each drug item.

The recorder could operate silently or it's speaker could be turned up to bellow out the conversation on the phone. Normally, the pharmacist turned the speaker down so he could hear the physician on the phone and not on the speaker.

I had just taken a call where I wanted the recorder's speaker to let me hear what was requested without me being close to the machine.

A second call came in from a doctor who had been asked to call us about one of his patients. The speaker was on full tilt. I was more than 30 feet from the speaker when his call came in. His patient was standing five feet from the speaker when the physician said, "What does that idiot hypochondriac want now? God, she is an impossible woman."

I flew to turn down the speaker, but the patient heard it all. She was furious. My apologies fell on deaf ears.

Our prescription bags featured photos of our pharmacists.
Eventually, we grew to 7 pharmacists.

Al Grube Timeline

1928   Born in Sheboygan, Wisconsin, on July 2.

1937   Father dies. Al and his mother move in with grandparents.

1940   Becomes newspaper delivery mogul, with 180 customers.

1942   Enters Central High School. Joins cheerleading squad. Works after school at Fessler Drug.

1945   Serves as First Semester All-School President. Loses bid for Valedictorian.

1946   Graduates from Central High School.

Enlists in the U.S. Army.

1947   Trains as an anti-aircraft artillery remote control system repairman. Serves as clerk-typist at Camp Stoneman, Calif.

Assigned to hospital ship Hope. Sails in the Pacific.

1948   Acquires hernia carrying drunk soldier. Has surgery at Letterman General Hospital, San Francisco.

Leaves the military.

Enrolls in UW-Madison, pre-pharmacy program.

1950   Urical cyst removed surgically, belly button lost.

1951   Joins the R.O.T.C. for officership in U.S. Army.

1952   Marries Marjory Panetti, college sweetheart, in October.

Graduates UW-Madison with a degree in pharmacy.

Passes pharmacy licensure exam.

Recalled to U.S. Army. Given state-side assignments.

1953   Assigned to Korea.

Daughter Lauren is born on April 10.

Returns to the U.S. in December, after Korean cease-fire

Moves his house trailer to Madison,

Marjory returns to school at UW-Madison.

1954   Enrolls in Laboratory Technician Training Program at Madison General Hospital.

Works nights for Rennebohm Drugs as a Reg. Pharmacist.

Al graduates from the Lab Tech Program in December.

1955   Signs with Walgreens to open an agency store in North gate Shopping Center in Sheboygan.

Moves house trailer to Chicago and works for Walgreens while Sheboygan store is being completed.

Moves to Sheboygan. Grube Drugs opens in the North-gate Shopping Center in October.

Daughter Lisa is born on December 23.

1956	Averages 100 hours of work a week for next three years.
1960	Joins Y's Men, a service club of the Y.M.C.A.
1961	Hires Phil Mersberger as a full-time pharmacist.
	Al works from 8 a.m. until noon as the hospital pharmacist for Plymouth Hospital, 12 miles west of Sheboygan, to help control costs and provide additional revenue.
1962	Leaves Y's men and joins Rotary.
1967	Builds in-ground swimming pool at his home.
1971	Opens a second Grube's Drug location on Sheboygan's south side.
1973	Opens a third pharmacy on Sheboygan's west side.
1975	Opens a pharmacy inside Morningside Nursing Home. Signs contract to supply all pharmaceuticals to their residents.
1976	Opens Paper Place card and gift store on 8th Street, managed by wife Marjory.
1977	Begins supplying all pharmaceuticals to residents of the Comprehensive Health Care Center.
1978	Closes pharmacy on west side.
	Adds Pine Haven Nursing Home to the pharmaceutical supply business.
1980	Opens Paper Place Too in Fond du Lac
	Contracts to be exclusive supplier of pharmaceuticals to the Sheboygan Retirement Home and Beech Health Care Center.
1981	Sells Grube Pharmacy on the south side.
1982	Divorces Marjory.
	Buys Evenson's Hallmark card and gift store in Memorial Mall.
1983	Marries the love of his life, Mary Lee Dickman on February 14, Valentine's Day. She becomes manager of the Hallmark store, now renamed Mary Lee's Hallmark.
	Sells Paper Place Too.
1984	Sunny Ridge Nursing Home, the area's largest, added to the pharmaceutical supply program.
1985	Closes Paper Place gift shop.
	Moves Northgate pharmacy to new space, doubling its size.
	Discontinues the senior citizen discount pharmacy inside Morningside Nursing Home.
1986	Opens pharmacy inside a Park and Shop supermarket.
1988	Serves as president of Wisconsin Pharmacy Assn, 2 yrs.
1997	Opens Deck the Halls Christmas store in April.
1999	Closes Deck the Halls in January, after the holiday season.

1999   Serves as president of Rotary in 1999 and 2000.

2001   Sells nursing home pharmaceutical supply business.

2002   Sells Grube Pharmacy Northgate to Aurora. Stays
        on to work for Aurora for one year.

2003   Retires at age 73.

2006   Sells Mary Lee's Hallmark store.

The Northgate store opened in 1955. The original store covered 5000 square feet. A
later move one door east doubled the size of the store.

The card and gift areas were carpeted to give a more plush feel.

Cards were an important contributor to our profit. "We cared enough to sell the very best"–Hallmark added class.

The prescription department was the center of our existence. When we had seven pharmacists on staff, we felt we had arrived.

Work: Ken Benson

Ken Benson's career is the topic of many sections in this book. This section includes material that add just a little more to the story of a farm boy from central Wisconsin who worked his way to the very top of two large corporations.

When it became known that Ken was resigning as Senior Vice-President of Kohler, his co-workers set up a mock ballot box and filled it with personal messages wishing him well. Before long, the box was removed by corporate officials who remain nameless, but somehow 70 ballots found their way to Ken. Here are two of them:

Bill Hanley led a campaign against Kohler Company's air pollution in the 1970s while a student at the nearby UW-Sheboygan Center. His article on Kohler's pollution got a state award for student newspapers. He was later hired by Kohler's advertising department after he finished college. Bill is a liberal Democrat.

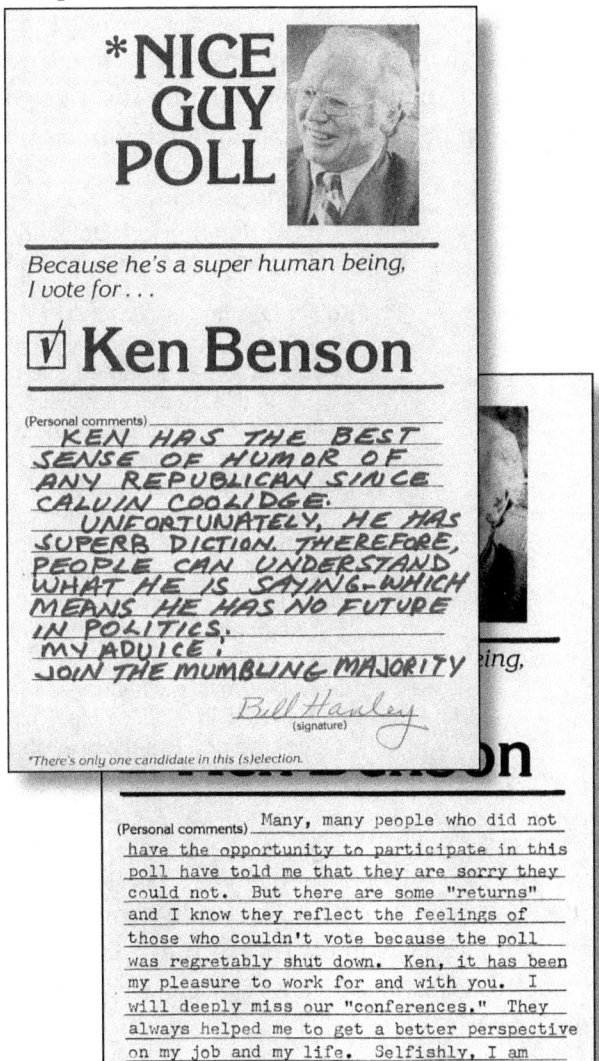

*NICE GUY POLL

Because he's a super human being, I vote for . . .

☑ **Ken Benson**

(Personal comments)

KEN HAS THE BEST SENSE OF HUMOR OF ANY REPUBLICAN SINCE CALVIN COOLIDGE. UNFORTUNATELY, HE HAS SUPERB DICTION. THEREFORE, PEOPLE CAN UNDERSTAND WHAT HE IS SAYING—WHICH MEANS HE HAS NO FUTURE IN POLITICS. MY ADVICE: JOIN THE MUMBLING MAJORITY

Bill Hanley
(signature)

*There's only one candidate in this (s)election.

(Personal comments) Many, many people who did not have the opportunity to participate in this poll have told me that they are sorry they could not. But there are some "returns" and I know they reflect the feelings of those who couldn't vote because the poll was regretably shut down. Ken, it has been my pleasure to work for and with you. I will deeply miss our "conferences." They always helped me to get a better perspective on my job and my life. Selfishly, I am sorry to see you leave but I know it is the best thing for you in the long picture. Keep us informed about your future. Best wishes from Bob & Edie Spatt.

Bob
(signature)

*There's only one candidate in this (s)election.

The Wall

On October 10, 1994, Ken had an appointment to pick up a witness fee at the Kohler Company Legal Department. His flight from North Carolina arrived early so he decided to visit the Kohler Design Center to kill time. He was surprised to see that the wall of company history made no reference to Walter Cleveland, former President of the company, Bill Doll, former Vice President of Sales and Marketing and Ken, former Senior Vice President. All three were all living former Kohler Company executives at that time.

Since then, some may have been reinstated to the wall. Ken was so amused by these omissions, that on his flight back to North Carolina that afternoon, he composed the following poem:

OFF THE WALL
By Ken Benson, October, 1994
(Dedicated to those who aren't on it.)

The Kohler Design Center Wall of Company history
To some is strangely cloaked in mystery.
Why are some proclaimed and others not?
Is this an evil Stalinist plot?
Name the second president with no Kohler name.
Why, Walter Cleveland bears that shame.
Who anonymously followed him as Senior V.P.?
Guess! (A clue: His initials are KVB.)
Who then became V.P. Marketing & Sales?
You're right! That's it! Bill Doll prevails!
Where are these loyal Company men who served for 40 years?
Alive and well, so have no fears!
They are vital and active, but share the fate
Of Kohler mystery history—a magic slate.
Did Doll stall? Did Walter falter? Did Ken B. fall?
Of course not! But they're "off the wall."

Graying Executives

About two years ago, Sally and I were dining at the Sheboygan Yacht Club. Just as we were departing, a handsome crew of sailors entered. I recognized them all. Terry Kohler, Tom Whidden, John Marshall, Pete Richlesdorfer, Chuck Lightcap, and Jay Hansen, were all attending a North Sails planning meeting.

After a brief bit of wool gathering and chatting about old times (it was more than ten years since I had served on the North Sails board of directors), I noticed that all but one of the men in the group had gray hair.

I commented about this phenomenon, "You guys have a management problem!" Jay Hansen was the only person who quietly nodded in agreement and smiled.

The Annual Meeting

Late in 1988, Terry Kohler was planning for the North Sails Annual Stockholders Meeting to be held in Miami, Florida.

The day before departure, Terry called Ken into his office and said, "Benson, you're going to have to fly to Miami and chair the North Sails Annual meeting for me, I've been subpoenaed to appear as a witness in a federal drug case in St. Louis."

Terry had previously assisted the FBI in catching a drug dealer by selling him the Vollrath Company's Learjet for cash. It all started when Tom Belot received a phone call from a man offering to buy the airplane, representing that his cash deal proposal would permit the Vollrath Company to evade federal income taxes. Tom immediately informed Terry of the call. They called the FBI, informing the agent of the illegal proposal. The FBI agent asked Terry to fly with him to Florida to close the deal and accept the cash in his presence. The drug dealer passed his briefcase full of bills to Terry and the agent made the arrest.

Terry had become the star witness in a federal tax law violation case against the drug dealer. Like in Al Capone's day, tax cases are easier to win than drug dealing cases. It was this case that abruptly interrupted Terry's North Sails Meeting just at the crucial time that he was going to introduce Tom Whidden as the new incoming President of North Sails. Tom had just returned from his America's Cup victory in New Zealand where he had served as tactician on Dennis Conner's 'Stars & Stripes' racing yacht.

Terry explained to Ken that Tom Whidden certainly shouldn't be saddled with running an annual meeting, which would be the very first North Sails meeting he had ever attended. Terry had recently appointed Tom President of North Sails after they met at the America's Cup races in Australia. Thus, there was no way Tom could comprehend whatever intricacies and intrigue might be going on within the North Sails organization.

I exclaimed, "Terry, things are pretty sad when we have reached the state where you are calling upon a former Juneau County dairy farmer with manure on his shoes and no sailing experience to run an annual North Sails Meeting attended by a bunch of clean, deck-shoed, champion, stockholding sailors."

The meeting, though heated at times, was held in Terry's absence. To this day, Tom Whidden holds the office of President of North Sails.

One page of a scrapbook given to Ken by his secretary at Kohler, Mildred Wieberdink. The scrapbook contained pages of doodles and scribbles made by Ken during business meetings. Unknown to Ken, Mildred retrieved the doodles from the circular file and saved them for the scrapbook.

In the dedication she wrote:
"During the years of serving as the secretary of Kenneth V. Benson, I have been a first-hand observer of both his managerial and personal characteristics and style. Because of the brilliance of some of the decisions made and the basis of the reasoning upon which they were formed, I felt I should pass on these gems of wisdom and profound observations to those who come after me. Therefore, I have compiled them and put them into a collection which can be a source of enlightenment to others as they pursue their careers."

Ken Benson Timeline

1929   Born in Mauston, Wisconsin on August 2.

1935   Begins public school in New Lisbon, Wisconsin, at The Little Red Schoolhouse.

1947   Graduates from New Lisbon High School as valedictorian, enters UW-Madison.

1950   Works summer jobs in North Dakota.

1951   Graduates from UW-Madison with a BA in Business Administration in January.

Marries Sally Drewry on June 23.

In the Army, leaves Ft. Riley, Kan., for Japan on July 19.

Arrives Yokohama harbor, Japan, on August 7, starts broadcasting from Radio Tokyo.

Transferred to Pusan, Korea, November 7.

1952   Sally sails to Japan on the "President Wilson" in October, joins Ken in Tokyo.

Ken and Sally leave Japan on a troop ship on Dec. 19.

1953   Ken and Sally arrive in Seattle on January 3, Ken is discharged from the army.

Moves to Appleton, Wisconsin, and joins the Marathon Corporation as a management trainee.

1954   Leaves Marathon in August, applies to Harvard Law School and is rejected.

Begins studies at the UW-Madison Law School in Sept.

1955   Daughter Jennifer is born on May 17.

1956   Elected vice-president of the American Law Student Association, Seventh Circuit.

1957   Daughter Elizabeth is born on March 4.

Graduates from UW-Madison Law School.

Starts law practice in Marshfield, Wisconsin, with classmate John Day, in July.

1958   Elizabeth severely injured after being run over by auto at her grandparents' farm on August 15.

Son Ken is born on August 22.

Answers a blind ad in the Wall Street Journal in December. Interviews with Mr. Chase at Kohler Company.

1959   Joins the legal department of Kohler on February 2.

Plays Drumond (Clarence Darrow) in the Sheboygan Players' "Inherit the Wind."

1960	Plays W. O. Gant in "Look Homeward Angel." Al Grube plays Luke Grant, his son.
1961	Son Jonathan is born on August 22.
1962	Has lead role in "Macbeth."
1963	Son Nathan is born on March 18.
1964	Chairman of the Bromley Humanities Seminar.
	Plays Anton Schill in "The Visit" opposite Marjory Grube.
	Plays Frank in "Take Her, She's Mine" opposite Virginia Garton.
1965	Plays Rubin Flood in "The Dark at the Top of the Stairs."
1966	Appointed assistant secretary of Kohler Company.
	Elected head of Sheboygan Community Players. Serves for two years.
1967	Sally's parents are both killed in an auto accident in Florida on February 7.
1968	Promoted to Secretary and Associate General Counsel of the Kohler Company in August.
1969	Named to Kohler's Board of Directors in March. Promoted to head of the Legal Dept. in September.
1971	Elected to Kohler's Executive Committee and appointed General Counsel in January.
	Daughter Jennifer is severely injured in an auto accident on October 31.
1972	Named a vice-president of the Kohler Co. in April.
1973	Elected to Board of Directors of Citizens Bank.
1974	Named Senior Vice-President of the Kohler Co. in March.
	Family trip to Sweden Norway and Denmark, July 7-29.
1975	Named to Board of Directors of Kohler de Mexico & Helvex.
1976	Temporarily managed Kohler International Ltd.
	Business trips to Mexico City, London, Singapore, Hong Kong and Japan in April, May, and June.
1979	Ran for U.S. Congress in the Republican primary, and lost, on February 20.
	Elected to Wigwam Co. board of directors in August.
1980	Named Senior Vice-President of Real Estate and Corporate Communications in May.
1982	Resigns from the Kohler Company on January 31.
	Joins the Vollrath Company as Vice-President of Corporate Development in April.
	Plays Norman Thayer, Jr., in "On Golden Pond."

1985   Elected President and Chief Operating Officer of the Vollrath Company in March.

1987   Named "Outstanding Alumni" by the University of Wisconsin Club of Sheboygan County.

1988   Plays the role of "Johnny Bull" at the J.M. Kohler Arts Center.

1989   Retires from Vollrath on Dec. 31 as the company reorganizes.

1990   Forms law firm in Sheboygan with Weldon Zufelt and Mary Lynn Donohue in January.

Plays Marius in "The Road to Mecca" at JMKAC.

Member of EnzoPac Co. board of directors as well as secretary and executive committee.

Member of Wisconsin 4-H Foundation board.

1991   Plays Weller Martin in "The Gin Game."

1992   Retires from Benson, Zufelt, and Donohue and moves to North Carolina.

1995   Appointed chairman of water study committee in Pine Knoll Shores, N.C. Sally and Ken travel to China.

1996   Elected senior warden of St. Francis by the Sea Episcopal Church in North Carolina.

Acted with Mary Doll in "Adam & Eve" and "Love Letters" in dinner theater performances in North Carolina.

Sally and Ken travel with Nate and Jessica to Sweden and England.

Sally and Ken attend the summer Olympics in Atlanta with Forer family and grandson, Carl.

1997   Travels the jungles of Uganda and Serengeti of Kenya.

1998   Began conducting Morning Prayer at Trinity Center, Pine Knoll Shores, North Carolina.

Sally & Ken travel by train from Beijing to Moscow; then on to St. Petersburg and England.

1999   Elected to the Board of Directors of Pine Knoll Shores Association.

2001   50th wedding anniversary celebration on June 23 at Jennifer's Blackstock house in Sheboygan.

Sally's brother George killed in auto accident on July 12.

2003   Joined St. Francis by the Sea choir. Volunteered as court-appointed Guardian ad Litum.

2004   Sally and Ken take a theater tour to London.

2005   Sally and Ken serve as Hospice volunteers in Carteret County, North Carolina

2007   Moves to Boise, Idaho, on January 1.

Community: Al Grube

Sheboygan, Wisconsin, is a city of about 50,000 people. It is where I was born and grew up. I found my way back home to practice my profession and own my own business.

It was easy to be interested in the community. I participated in many community projects and was active in Y's Men and a Rotary. I served my profession by being active in the state pharmacy association.

My regret is that I could have done more, but the long hours I spent in my pharmacy did hold me back.

Y's Men

Each of us have an obligation to help make our community a better place. It's always tempting to leave that responsibility to the other guy, but it is gratifying to look back and say because of my efforts it became possible to have this park, or a better police department, or a more effective school system, or some other community improvement.

Many good things in our communities exist because a group of interested citizens pooled their efforts to make it happen.

The YMCA in our community has a group of folks called Y's Men, who try to make the Sheboygan YMCA the best it can be. For a number of years I was active and can look back now and say some of my efforts helped to make the Y's programs some of the best in our area.

One of their fund raisers was to sell Christmas trees. I participated for a number of years until one Christmas season I came down with a bad cold which kept me from giving full effort to my own business. The monetary loss I took that season convinced me that this fund raiser was not practical for me. Conveniently, another service club was soliciting my membership, and I decided to switch my affiliation.

I remained a dues-paying member of the Y for several decades in spite of never using its facilities.

Here Again

Fund drives are done by every imaginable nonprofit known to man and believe me, once you are on the fund raising circuit, everyone calls you to perform. I am convinced the groups share their names with each other with the hope that once involved you can be counted on to render the same service to their group when asked.

For a number of years it was the same groups that called me. But toward the end, it seemed every group had my name, and expected me to serve.

One week I had been out for three different groups in the same week when I stopped at the office of an acquaintance who complained, "Al, you have been here three times this week already. I'm not going to let you in if you come again." It was his challenge that brought home to me that I was spending too much of my working hours on fund raising. I made the decision I would contact every group I had collected for in the previous six months and inform them that I was going to take a two-year sabbatical and concentrate on my business.

I refused all requests for two years. In the last 30 years I haven't been asked again and I now concentrate my free time on organizations I hold membership in. The number of groups raising funds has forced a lot of generous people to restrict their giving to groups who are serving their own needs or have an existing situation close to them.

Rotary

It has always seemed to me that Rotary has a diversified list of worthwhile causes and that they do a good job of keeping their memberships involved in not only community projects, but also international concerns as well.

The Salvation Army has always been a pet project of our Downtown Sheboygan Rotary Club. Each Christmas, my fellow Rotarians ring bells for the Salvation Army and collect a sizable sum of money for them. At least two decades have gone by in which our club has kept the traveling trophy for collecting the most funds of our local service clubs.

I had the privilege of serving our club as president. It was both rewarding and trying. When the year was over, I felt, like many of my past president friends, that "I really was happy and committed to serve, but I don't feel I can spare another year to do it again."

One wonderful memory from the year of my presidency was our International Convention held in Singapore. My predecessor went to Kansas City and the gentleman who followed me went to Chicago. I cannot help but feel I was blessed. Mary and I were adopted in Singapore by a group from Hawaii, and our non-meeting times were special to both of us.

Community: Ken Benson

Ken believed strongly in serving his community. During the 33 years that Sally and Ken lived in Sheboygan County, he served on various boards including The Sheboygan Chamber of Commerce, Sheboygan United Way, Kiwanis Club, Sheboygan YMCA (secretary, vice president), Lakeland College Board of Trustees, Sheboygan Community Players (president), Sheboygan Retirement Home (president), St Luke United Methodist Church (chairman of the administrative board), Sheboygan County Bar Association (president), Wisconsin 4-H Foundation, Sheboygan County Republican Party (membership chairman and member of the executive committee), The Bromley Humanities Seminar (chairman), and the Grace Episcopal Church Vestry (senior warden).

After Ken and Sally moved to Pine Knoll Shores, North Carolina, he served on the vestry of St. Francis by the Sea Episcopal Church as Senior Warden and also chaired its capital campaign for building the church. Sally served as chairman of the building committee and was the vestry's contract representative in building the church. They were also both volunteers with Hospice.

Ken was active in community theater in Sheboygan, starting in the late 1950s. In 1988, the *Sheboygan Press* published this article about how his business career and his favorite hobby were related:

Theater, business, creative mix for Ken Benson

by Natalie Johnson, the *Sheboygan Press,* July 3, 1988.

The dramatic and creative elements of the theater seem far removed from the world of a corporate executive, but for Kenneth Benson, president and chief executive officer of the Vollrath Company and veteran actor with the Sheboygan Community Players, the two are less dissimilar than at first thought.

Pure and simple, "theater helps me be a better businessman," commented Benson, who has played many varied parts including Clarence Darrow in "Inherit the Wind," in 1959, the lead role in "Macbeth" in 1962, and Norman in "On Golden Pond" in 1982. He also served as president of the Community Players from 1966 to 1968.

In his office at the Vollrath Company decorated with artwork and framed photos from his performance as Macbeth, Benson compared the sensitivity one needs to relate to employees as similar to the sensitivity necessary to create a character.

In theater, "you have to create an illusion of the first time and a reality for the audience on the stage," he explained. He stressed the teamwork involved in trying to give the perfect performance by not breaking the illusion. From the director and the actors to the stage manager, properties manager, interns and light technicians, everyone plays a part in creating the illusion. "It all has to knit together under intense pressure."

In business, according to Benson, you plan your time and hire good people who follow your plan. In the end, "you have more time to act," said Benson.

Thursday, Benson will take the stage again playing "a crude tough SOB" in the play, "Johnny Bull," at the John Michael Kohler Arts Center. With a short rehearsal time of two weeks, the practices are intense, as is the play.

A certain camaraderie takes over the casts Benson has worked with. "Titles and stations in life are of no consequence, because it is what you do and how you relate in the production that counts."

Benson recalls one play in which in real life one actor was on parole, the make-up artist was a policewoman and Benson was the vice-president of Kohler Company. "In amateur theater you work with a cross section of the community for a goal that enriches everyone."

At the end of a play's performance run, Benson said that on one hand, he feels relief that it is over, but on the other hand there is a sense of nostalgia for the cast and crew.

Theater has been an important part of Benson's life since high school, where he was involved in forensics and theater. He actually started out as a speech and drama major at the University of Wisconsin-Madison where he worked for the school's radio station. "It's been with me always," said Benson, "but I got disgustingly practical and went into business."

Through a stint in the army in Korea and his career as a lawyer and business executive, his interest in theater has stayed alive. Because of his busy schedule, Benson doesn't participate constantly in community theater. He explains he has been "bitten by a bug that can go into remission, but will come out periodically."

Macbeth was the "hardest thing I ever tried to do," Benson said modestly. His favorite part was in "Inherit the Wind." While his interest in the theater and the amount of time he has to do such activities sometimes do not coincide, "I don't expect my interest in drama to diminish." Benson smiled as he said, "theater is my golf game."

In *Light up the Sky,* 1960, Ken played a Shriner. Mary Dwyre and Marjory Grube were part of the cast.

The Country Girl, 1966, Ken and Roger Fischer. Ken played the Bing Crosby role.

On Golden Pond, 1982, starred Ken Benson and Mary Garton.

from the Sheboygan Press,
February 19, 1970 issue:

Benson-Grube Duo Make 'Lion' Roar

by Shirley Jarvis

"The Lion in Winter" could have been written for Marjory Grube and Kenneth Benson. The play has the virility and power that these two deserve. But, artists that they are, they . . . go on to explore, to innovate, to enrich, to probe the roles of Henry II and Eleanor of Aquitaine until they emerge like many-faceted jewels—magnetic, compelling, fascinating.

There are moments of sheer magic as the two Sheboygan Players veterans take the play in their teeth and shake it until it crackles with intensity.

Ken as Henry II, King of England, and Marjory Grube as his wife, Eleanor of Aquitaine.

THE SHEBOYGAN COMMUNITY PLAYERS
present

THE LION IN WINTER

by James Goldman
Production Directed by David C. Bryant

Set Design by Suzanne Bauer   Costume Design by Patricia Von Rautenkranz

CAST

Alais Capet, a French Princess ....Cherry Van Kirk
Henry II, King of England.. Kenneth V. Benson
Prince John, the youngest son .... Richard Demeuse
Prince Geoffrey, Duke of Brittany, the middle son .... Ralph Van Kirk
Prince Richard, the Lion Hearted, the oldest son ....Thomas Zientek
Eleanor of Aquitaine, Henry's wife.................................... Marjory Grube
Philip Capet, King of France.......................,.................. Jean-Paul Alegre
Stand-bys ....Karin Schreiber, Kenneth Binder

The Time: Christmas, 1183

Ken had the lead role in "Macbeth", presented by the Community Players in 1962. Marjory Grube played Lady Macbeth.

Jean Bryant and Ken Benson starred in *The Gin Game*.

Mary Doll as Eliza Gant, scolds Ken Benson, as W. O.
Gant, her husband in "Look Homeward, Angel."

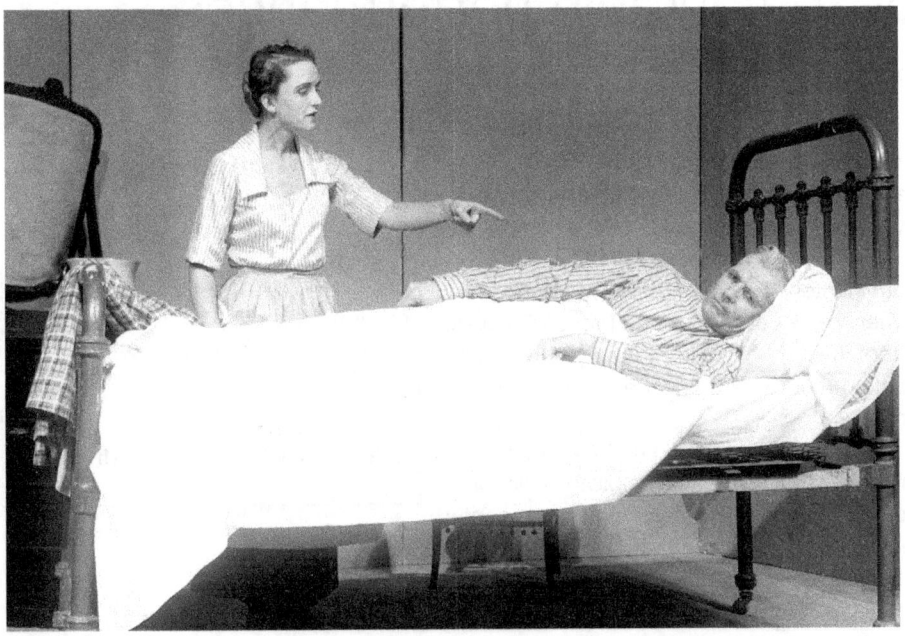

THE COMMUNITY PLAYERS OF SHEBOYGAN

present

"Look Homeward, Angel"

by Ketti Frings

Based on the Novel
by Thomas Wolfe

Production directed by David C. Bryant

Designed by John Posewitz

CAST:

Ben Gant	Don Rintz
Mrs. Marie "Fatty" Pert	Belle Whiffen
Helen Gant Barton	Laury Wehner
Hugh Barton	Arnold Rhiel
Eliza Gant	Mary Doll
W. O. Gant	Kenneth V. Benson
Dr. Maguire	Arno Roehl
Madame Elizabeth	Dorothy Hennell
Luke Gant	Alfred Grube

Ken and Al were both in the cast of "Look Homeward Angel,"
presented by the Sheboygan Players in 1960. Ken played the
abusive father, Al played his son.

'Road to Mecca' highlighted by remarkable performances

by Marion Stewart, in the Sheboygan Press

The John Michael Kohler Art Center's Summer Theater production of the Athol Fugard play is lit by remarkable performances by Barbara Bassewitz, Ken Benson and Julie Scattergood. They are out of the ordinary, both in intensity and complexity.

Benson, as the Reverend Marius Byleveld, offers the kind of performance you wish you could run backward and watch again and again.

Benson's performance makes Fugard's grasp of complexity accessible. . . Benson conveys the conflicts, fears and deep-seated feeling of this complex man brilliantly, and when he leaves the stage, you feel loss.

The Road To Mecca

by Athol Fugard
Directed by Jonathan Smoots

The Cast

Helen. . . . . Barbara Bassewitz
Marius . . . Ken Benson
Elsa. . . . . . Julie Scattergood

Time: Autumn 1974
Place: New Bethesda, South Africa

Love Letters

by A.R. Gurney; directed by Laura Kohler

Andrew Makepeace Ladd III   Ken Benson
Melissa Gardner   Mary Garton

Stage Manager   Audrey Waitkus
Lighting Design   Eric R. Johnson

There will be a 15-minute intermission.
A reception for the performers will follow the opening night performance.

They meet in second grade.
Their love lasts a lifetime.
They can't live together.
They can't live apart.
They write letters. . .
for fifty years. . .

In the early 1960's Mary Garton and her husband, Bob were neighbors to Sally and Ken. In May of 1962, Mary portrayed one of the three witches in Macbeth. In 1982 Mary and Ken enjoyed playing the lead roles in "On Golden Pond."

Mary was founder of the John Michael Kohler Arts Foundation. She wanted to perform on the stage of the John Michael Kohler Arts Center Theatre. In December of 1993 she persuaded Ken to return to Sheboygan from North Carolina for their performance of "Love Letters," under the direction of Laura Kohler. Mary was 77 years old.

from the Sheboygan Press in 1986:

Benson to Get 4-H Alumni Award

A veteran Sheboygan area industrialist and civic leader will be honored in Madison Tuesday evening as a Wisconsin 4-H alumni. Kenneth V. Benson is one of three 4-H alumni being singled out for recognition at a program held in conjunction with the 1986 State 4-H Congress.

Benson was a 4-H member in Juneau County from 1940 to 1946, participating in such projects as dairy, gardening and leadership.

Benson reflected on his years of 4-H membership: "4-H work as a child taught me both discipline and the importance of quality work," said Benson, "and permitted me to experience the reward of success. Truly, head, heart, hands and health have been a significant part of my life."

While serving as a corporal in the U. S. Army in Korea in 1951, Benson became so concerned about the youth of the country that he tried to reactivate its 4-H movement. He discussed 4-H on three radio programs and worked with the director of the Korean National 4-H club to translate a 75-page 4-H leadership publication into Korean. He later convinced the U. S. military to print 200,000 copies of the booklet, then organized a leadership training session on how to start 4-H clubs in Korea.

In a letter to a superior, Corporal Benson wrote, "Why not try to get some spirit into farm life by a nationwide coverage of 4-H clubs? Here is an idea . . . that could do more good than all the dollar aid that has been poured into Korea."

Benson and his wife, Sally, live near Oostburg. All five of his children have been 4-H members in Sheboygan County.

In his first career as lawyer in Marshfield, Ken got involved in community service. He served as chairman of the area's March of Dimes campaign, raising money to fight polio. This photo from the Marshfield News-Herald shows Ken and Marian Graff preparing coin cards for distribution.

Book Two: Achieving the Dreams

1. Vision
2. Mission
3. Candor in Communications
4. Trust
5. Commitment
6. Spirit
7. Monitor
8. Measuring Goals
9. Fair Compensation
10. Profit

The Ten Principles

Our original goal in writing this book was to select ten critical factors that would impact the bottom line of any business. These factors were something like the Ten Commandments; ten things to do that will make every company a better place to work and will lead to greater profitability.

When Moses delivered God's Ten Commandments to the people of Israel, he told them to listen to all the laws, learn them and obey them. The people of Israel were to learn two things from these commandments: their duty to God (the first four commandments) and their duty to their neighbors (the last six commandments).

While it is not our intent to imply that this brief book should rise to the level of a Biblical mandate, we do want to clearly distinguish our first six chapters in Book Two from the next four. The first six chapter titles deal with the moral, spiritual and philosophical flywheel which will successfully power the business in the right direction over the long term. The remaining four chapters pertain more to the mechanics, measurement and numbers of the business to make it profitable.

1. Vision

Vision is the picture of your dream that has the potential to fulfill your future goals.

A vision is a dream. It is the outcome if all goes as desired. The vision is not what was, nor what is, but what can be. The size of the vision determines the future significance of the visionary.

There are many ways to say "the buck stops here." But the fact remains—there is one leader. That leader must have a vision. That vision will propel the business or project forward, or into a state of change. Without the vision, the entity will become stagnant and decline. Visions are fluid; they can be modified, changed, or abandoned. It is the vision that provides direction for the enterprise.

Once the vision has been expressed, there must be a reality check of what can be accomplished. You must take individual steps to attain the vision. Each step in the process must be fulfilled before starting the next step. The first step is to set a foundation upon which future steps will be built.

Your vision for your business is a precursor of a mission statement for that business, the subject of the next chapter. The business mission statement must be consistent with your vision and should permit fulfillment of your vision.

Your vision will remain a dream until you act upon it. Refine your vision, put it in writing, get advice from others. Once refined, divide your vision into segments, put deadlines on the segments, then begin to complete each segment. Prioritize and determine which segment comes first, the time required to complete it, and the things required to effectively do the job.

Smaller to larger segments are preferable; the reward of completion is important for your psyche. Early in your work you should experience and enjoy a sense of accomplishment.

How do you decide on a vision? Remember, it is a dream, an idea that rolls around in your mind that represents improvement. Things will be better, more effective, cheaper, easier to use, or just plain neater. There are no limits to what you can dream. It is helpful to digress, and ask yourself, "What was?" Then be sure you know "What is?" and your question to yourself then should be "What can be?"

There is absolutely nothing that cannot be improved in some way, whether it's a product, a person, or an enterprise. Everything can be made better in some way, shape, or form. Whether it's size, price, speed, versatility, or other advantages, everything can be made better, more effective, or somehow, some way improved giving rise to another goal.

Your vision is the motivation for a fuller life.

Al's Clear Vision

Al's example of his personal vision might be found in his own life. He dreamed of someday owning a chain of drugstores. He was serving in the military as World War II was ending when he had this vision of his future.

To achieve his vision, it seemed prudent for Al to become a pharmacist. His first goal was to get a degree in pharmacy, then pass the state licensing exams, then find a job as a registered pharmacist. This required selecting a college, being accepted by that college, and pushing himself to adapt to the need for learning so that he might qualify for an internship. Al needed to learn the mechanical skills as well as fulfill the academic requirements so that academics and practice together would qualify him to pass the state board exams to get licensed.

Once his license was in hand, his next goal was to select a site for his future practice, and find a way to accumulate the resources to start that practice. Then, and only then, could he begin.

Al's vision of drugstore ownership came about in a somewhat unusual way. He had met the goals of graduation from pharmacy school and he had successfully passed his internship and board exams. His credentials were all in order, but the Korean War intervened and once again Al was privileged to serve his country, spending several months being moved about the U.S., and finally making an appearance in Korea.

Serving as a second lieutenant convinced Al that his original dream was far more appealing than a military career. Once again he revised his vision; this time abandoning the chain concept, deciding instead on having a clinical pharmacy and clinical lab combination.

To become credentialed for this clinical laboratory assignment required a certification in medical technology and additional schooling. Al enrolled in a Med Tech program at the Madison General Hospital using his GI benefits and worked in a pharmacy in Madison.

During his training, Al found time to seek and find a location for his proposed venture. A pharmacy owner in Wisconsin Dells had passed his 65th birthday and had no interested heirs to replace him. A land contract with Al was acceptable to the owner. The contract payments would supplement the owner's retirement savings.

The location was ideal. This small community had a small hospital that would benefit greatly from a clinical pharmacy. The hospital's pathologist was one of Al's educators. He agreed to serve as Al's professional counselor. This fulfilled the hospital society's requirement of oversight by a Board certified pathologist.

Al lived with his dream for months—almost to graduation from the Med Tech program; then his dream was shattered because the planned location became unavailable.

Al was depressed. But then he received a phone call from his mother. She asked him to go to Sheboygan, his former home, to negotiate a real estate transaction for her. Al arrived early for his Sheboygan appointment. To kill time, he drove around the city. He saw a sign on a vacant lot on the north side of Sheboygan announcing the development of a small shopping center to be completed within the year. The developer was planning for a Walgreen Agency drugstore to be located in the middle of the shopping center. This potential drugstore would be located in an attractive site between the two major anchors, a large supermarket and a Penney's store.

Al called the real estate developer and asked to meet with him. It turned out to be a serendipitous meeting because at that very moment a Walgreens representative was in town, meeting with the developer. The representative had the authority to decide which pharmacist would represent Walgreens. The sales pitch Al received from the developer and the Walgreens representative convinced him that this was his opportunity of a lifetime.

The Walgreens representative's one concern was that Al's prior experience was only with Rexall drugstores or independents. Al knew nothing about Walgreens products or their systems. This barrier was overcome when Al learned he could work in Chicago as a pharmacist for Walgreens. He could also visit the Walgreens Chicago national headquarters any time he wished. All Al had to do was move to Chicago and become a pharmacist with Walgreens while the Sheboygan store was under construction.

Al's move was simple. He owned a house trailer; Walgreens found a trailer park in the Chicago suburbs. Since Al was a licensed pharmacist in Wisconsin, licensure reciprocity required a simple interview followed by immediate approval by the State of Illinois. Al was now ready to start work the very next day as a fully registered Illinois pharmacist.

Al's compensation matched his counterparts. He developed a lifelong respect for the Walgreen Company. He had been given a great and broadening experience. Unfortunately, a number of years later the Walgreens hierarchy abandoned its Agency division. Had that not happened, Al would probably have stayed with Walgreens until he retired.

What did Al learn?

1) Dreams can be fluid; they can change.

2) Your vision can take on a direction of its own.

3) Your personal confidence and decision-making skills may encounter a change in timing which could even possibly change your future.

Once Al's direction was established, his next step became clear. He established a successful business mission statement with the collaboration of his associates.

Pursuing his dream provided Al with 45 happy and fulfilling years with an income that provided for his life's desires. Currently, Al is enjoying his retirement without concern and his wants and needs are met. His lifestyle is simple, but international travel is not prohibitive, so Al enjoys both worlds. He lives simply, but is able to spice up his life with foreign travel, whether its biking in Europe or cruising the Mediterranean. It is all possible.

Ken's Career: A capsule of a cloudy vision

Ken's vision as to what he was about and where he was going was cloudier than Al's.

His first experience in business took place on his father Carl's dairy farm near New Lisbon, Wisconsin. Carl was a thrifty Swedish dairy farmer. He had struggled through the 1929 depression, almost losing his heavily mortgaged farm. By the early 1940's Carl had made a comeback and had built up his herd to about twenty-five Holstein purebreds. He proudly showed his animals at county fairs in Mauston and Elroy. He also showed his prize bull, Inka May, at the Wisconsin State Fair in Milwaukee. Carl was pleased that Inka won second place, beaten only by the first-place bull from Maytag farms of the state of Washington. Carl proudly proclaimed that his bull was the best bull of its class in Wisconsin.

By the time he was twelve, Ken was milking cows, cleaning barns, driving horses, driving tractor, helping work the land and harvesting the crops. He was a member of a 4-H club and had as many as six calves for 4-H projects. He also showed Holstein cattle at the county fair in Mauston.

At the end of each year Ken had to complete his 4-H record books, accounting for all the details of his project activities; this was not his favorite part of 4-H work.

When Ken was about thirteen years old, his father told him he could pick out any heifer calf in the pen as his very own. Carl explained to Ken that when the heifer matured and was a milk cow, he could keep any of the net proceeds from the sale of her milk after deducting purchased feed costs. Ken's pick was a good one. He named the calf Becky and showed her for several years at the county fairs, always getting a blue ribbon. Not only that, Becky became the most productive cow in the herd. Ken saved the monthly money he received from her daily milk sales.

Ken, age 15, and his Holstein, Becky, at the Juneau County Fair in Mauston. Becky won many blue ribbons. Ken saved the proceeds from Becky's milk sales for his college fund.

Leaving the farm

In the spring of 1947, when Ken was a senior in high school, he decided to go on to college. His sister, Mil, encouraged him. Being an only son, he reluctantly informed his father of his plans. Ken could have taken over the family farm upon high school graduation, following the footsteps of his father. But this was not Ken's vision of his future. Instead, he chose to further his education.

When Ken told his dad that he wanted to attend the University of Wisconsin, Carl sold his 160-acre farm for $16,000. He had a dispersal sale of his entire purebred Holstein herd that July. Carl did not complain about his son's decision. Becky was the highest-priced animal sold at the dispersal sale. She sold for $500. Ken added these proceeds to his accumulated savings from the sale of Becky's milk; the total–$1,200. Carl didn't offer Ken any further financial help. Later, Carl loaned Ken $400 in his senior year in college. Ken paid his father back several years later.

First tries at a career

Ken was discharged from the army in January, 1953, and he and Sally moved to Appleton, Wisconsin. He was employed by Marathon Corporation as a management trainee in nearby Menasha. The Marathon training program rotated trainees from job to job throughout the company. Managers were permitted to interview trainees for a full-time assignment. If a trainee received an offer, he could decide whether or not he wished to take the job. After six months in the training program, Ken accepted a job as a sales correspondent with the meat and vegetable oil division. He entered orders for printed food packages and served as liaison between customer, salesman and the factory.

Ken felt underpaid and overburdened as he watched over several millions of dollars worth of printed meat and vegetable oil cartons. His starting pay was $272 per month. By the time he left the company in August of 1954, he was earning $375 per month.

Ken and Sally decided to drive to Boston, Massachusetts. Ken had applied to take the Foreign Service exams there and also decided to explore the possibility of attending Harvard Law School. Ken's Harvard interview was the shortest on record. Mr. Pfeifer, the Assistant Dean, asked Ken what he wanted; Ken said he wanted to apply for admission to Harvard Law School. "Do you want to be a lawyer?" asked Mr. Pfeifer. Ken replied, "I don't know." Mr. Pfeifer responded, "We don't want you."

The three-and-one-half day written Foreign Service exam proved equally unsatisfactory. A score of 70 was required to move upward to the next step. Ken's score was 68.

A few weeks later in September of 1954, Ken began his studies at the University of Wisconsin Law School.

A seminar of top politicians

In law school, Ken was active in student organizations. He represented the University of Wisconsin at the 7th circuit meeting of the American

Law Student Association and was elected vice-president of the 7th circuit, which covered Wisconsin, Illinois, Iowa, and Indiana. Earlier, Ken was elected to the board of the UW Law School Student Association. This election resulted in the UW Law School hosting the annual meeting of the members of the 7th Circuit American Law Student Association. As chairman of the meeting, Ken arranged for a seminar entitled, "The Lawyer and Politics." Participants in the program were State Senator Gaylord Nelson (later elected U.S. Senator), State Senator Warren Knowles (later elected Governor of Wisconsin), and James Doyle, then a resentative of the U.S. State

Ken Benson and Jim Brewer represented Wisconsin at the 7th circuit American Law Student Association convention held at the UW Law school in 1957. Benson is the retiring circuit vice-president. *From the Advocate, a newspaper of the UW Law School, June, 1957:*

Department, later appointed a U.S. District Judge. Doyle is the father of Jim Doyle, currently the Governor of Wisconsin.

The law practice

Ken graduated from law school in June of 1957. By then, he and Sally were the proud parents of Jennifer and Elizabeth. Ken and a classmate, John Day, obtained a veteran's loan from the State of Wisconsin and purchased a defunct law practice in Marshfield. A fresh new sign appeared on the office: "Benson & Day, Attorneys at Law." Clients were not plentiful. Ken would borrow money, give half of the proceeds to John; then they would buy groceries for their families, paying the rent for another month.

A help wanted ad in the Wall St. Journal

Although the law practice was growing, it was not maturing fast enough to pay off the debt and provide for two families. Ken suggested to John that his marketing degree was more relevant to employment than John's history major from UW Platteville. It seemed logical for Ken to take the first step in searching for a job elsewhere while they both continued to expand their law practice. Ken answered a blind ad in the Wall Street Journal. Lucius P. Chase, Vice President and General Counsel of Kohler Company responded to Ken's brief letter and resume. Ken and Sally drove to Kohler, Wisconsin, for the job interview. Kohler was located only twelve miles from Sally's parents' farm in Sheboygan County.

Ken was offered a job as an attorney in Kohler's legal department. He began his new job on February 2, 1959. He worked directly for Mr. Chase as the only additional attorney in the legal department. Gelane Grainger served as secretary to both Mr. Chase and Ken. That was it. Three people constituted the Kohler Company legal department.

Rapid rise and abrupt end

About six years later, Ken was promoted to Assistant Secretary of Kohler Company. In March of 1969 he was elected to the Board of Directors and appointed Secretary of the company. In 1972 Ken became Vice President and General Counsel. Two years later, he was promoted to Senior Vice President. In this new position, the General Counsel, Secretary, Vice President of Finance, Vice President of Industrial Relations, Director of Advertising, Director of Public Affairs and the Internal Auditor all reported to him. Later, he became responsible for Kohler's real estate and its new hospitality division which included the Sports Core, American Club, River Wildlife, Kohler farms and Kohler stables, as well as other real estate development and planning. Ken served on the Kohler Company Executive Committee, Real Estate Committee, and Pension Planning Committee.

On January 31, 1982, Ken resigned from the Kohler Company.

He had worked for Kohler Co. for twenty-three years, except for a brief absence without pay when he unsuccessfully ran for Congress after the December 4, 1978 death of Bill Steiger. This special primary election was held on February 20, 1979. Ken was among seven other Republican candidates, which included Tommy Thompson who later became Wisconsin's governor. Ken ran as a "non politician," and proved it by losing. Tom Petri won the primary and defeated Gary Goyke, his Democrat opponent. Tom has served continuously since then as Congressman for the Sixth District.

"I'm Not A Politician..."

BENSON FOR CONGRESS

▶ "I'm not a politician and I think that's an advantage today. Voters are tired of politicians who always compromise . . . and end up voting for bad legislation that causes higher taxes or more bureaucratic government. I think I'm equipped to make the tough decisions that really are in the people's best interest. My legal experience and my business background helps. I'm used to making decisions and to managing operations and money effectively. We certainly can use more of that in government today."

▶ "It would be impetuous of me to say I have solutions to all the Nation's problems. In fact, anyone who says they do isn't the person you want in Congress. I will work hard, study the issues, and make the best decisions I can for the people of the 6th District and the country."

BENSON cares

▶ "I hope to get broad-based support from the entire area . . . not just Sheboygan County or Juneau County where I was born. I worked in Menasha and, over the past 20 years, I've traveled the entire District and made many friends among laborers, farmers, senior citizens and ethnic groups . . . people from all walks of life."

New career

After resigning from the Kohler Company, Ken accepted an offer from Terry Kohler, and on April 1, 1982, became Vice President of Corporate Development of Vollrath Company and a member of its Board of Directors. He was elected President of the company in March, 1985. Vollrath Company was decentralized on December 31, 1989 and became a holding company named Windway Capital Corporation. Ken and Weldon Zufelt, formerly General Counsel of Kohler and later of Vollrath Company, became law partners in January of 1990. They were also counsel and advisors to Windway. Within a few months, Mary Lynn Donohue became their third partner, the firm was named "Benson, Zufelt & Donohue". Ken retired in 1992 when the firm was dissolved. He and Sally moved to North

Carolina that August.

The flexible vision

The critical point of vision is reality. Flexibility is essential, and the willingness to adapt can and will guarantee success and life fulfillment. To be intractable means failure can occur. You must be willing to commit to a different venture if the chips are falling against you.

Your vision is absolutely essential to success, but to conclude only one path exists is tantamount to accepting failure. Al and Ken envisioned different directions, and yet they both experienced happiness, fulfillment, and some economic success in the paths they followed.

Vision is your dream for the future, created in your mind to, in some way, improve something that exists. You must determine your own steps to make your vision a reality. This vision becomes possible when you define the steps to be taken and assign a timeline to those steps and take one step at a time. Only when your vision becomes a reality, can you step back and enjoy your accomplishments.

You cannot sit down and intellectually state, "I am going to have a vision." It must be instinctive. You have observed a process that can be improved. It could be a product, a person, or an enterprise. You are convinced it can be improved in some way, shape, or form. It may be improved in size, price, cost, speed, versatility, or whatever. You can make it better and you determine how that can be done.

We believe you can develop this skill by getting in the habit of trying to do every task you are assigned better. Share your thoughts with your superior, you will become the "go-to" guy, and your advancement will be assured.

2. Mission

*Mission is the planned direction to achieve the goals
your vision has established.*

Every business must have a mission. Contemplate your vision, then determine what must be done to make that vision a reality. The mission should be described in a mission statement which states what you want your business to be remembered for. It spells out the reason you are in business, what you want to accomplish, the reason your clients or customers come to you and the justification for your economic existence. Your mission should create standards that can be appreciated by all who give you the honor and respect of their business.

Your mission statement can provide the motivation to make your business a viable economic entity. Without a clear mission, you bumble along without direction, attempting to be all things to all people. Without clear direction, change becomes a constant, continuity does not exist, economic rewards are small, and emotional rewards are almost nonexistent.

To define your mission statement, first consider your vision. What principles must be followed in the mission statement to make your vision come to fruition? What must I do to be different and unique? You should try to be superior to your competitors in some way.

In Al's case, his pharmacy was similar to others in his market area. His services were mandated by existing laws, and long-established professional practices. Yet, there had to be something he could do to make his business stand out from his competition. There had to be something to give him the edge over the others.

Al's mission statement read:

"We are a Model of Quality and Service, Treating our Customers and Associates as Friends."

The mission statement sounds simple. But, to be effective, a mission must be fully internalized by both yourself and your associates, living it and understanding it 24/7. This is surprisingly difficult.

Quality in products and service requires constant attention to detail. The marketplace is full of good deals; the problem becomes one of high standards. Does the product or service meet your high standards? Are you sure? Is the reputation of your provider above reproach? How can you prove that to yourself? What do you do if your evaluation is flawed and you discover problems? You are exposed to economic loss if you correct them, and yet it is possible your buyer is not even aware that something is wrong. At this point your integrity is up for challenge. How will you respond?

The quality and benefits of your products and services should be sufficiently understated in a way that pleasantly surprises the customer. The goal is not only to meet expectations, but to exceed them. Everyone in the business must adhere to high standards no matter what their job.

The mission takes on the position of a mantra, practiced with a zealousness that fosters dedication that can only be interpreted as your organization's desire to be the very best.

Al's mission statement emphasized treating both customers and associates as friends. This forced him to be kind, considerate, helpful, and understanding, always giving everyone the benefit of the doubt. The essence of this position is you must get to know and appreciate your customers and your associates.

Al believes a successful mission statement must be broad, basic, short, doable, and easy to remember. Then you must use it, repeat it often, and reward your associates whenever they apply it.

While any business should develop a mission statement that is the work product of all of its key executives, it cannot deviate from the broad vision of its owner if it is to be successfully implemented.

The development of a mission statement should not be rushed. It can be best accomplished by spending several days with key executives as they analyze and express what seems to be working and not working within the business. Only after exchanging views in depth and candor and assessing what the business should be doing and how to correct what it isn't doing, can the executives start work on the mission statement itself. This mission statement should clearly articulate the broad purpose of the business in its simplest terms.

The mission statement should be a memorable, creative product of all of the participants. It should have the total commitment of its creators. The company executives must inform, teach and encourage all employees of the business to understand the mission statement and its importance as the first part of any future planning. Everyone in the business should know what the mission statement means. They, in turn should develop their own specific strategic and short-term plans within the scope of the mission statement. Without universal understanding of the business mission statement, the business will lose focus. If a mission statement does not successfully filter out the irrelevant, it deserves no further consideration and should be summarily dismissed and reworked.

The mission statement should not be changed quickly or easily. It is the broad, long-term present and future path for the business. The mission statement should be reviewed each year, but not changed unless the key executives understand that a change in mission may be a radical change of direction for the company. Since employees and executives come and go through the life of a business, it is important that all new employees have the opportunity to learn about the mission statement and its importance. Without this continuity, the company mission will fail.

It is apparent that Al had a clearly focused vision of what he was about in life. Ken did not. The distinction between Al's focus and Ken's diffuse approach are simple. Al had a vision of owning and operating his own business. Here a simple vision of the concept would do the job. Al had a vision and he worked directly with his associates to create a mission statement that would fulfill his vision.

Al had a vision of ownership. Ken did not. Ken was actually a hired gun that assisted in developing mission statements of companies owned by others. Anyone owning and operating a business should seek the participation of all of its employees to fulfill the owner's vision by developing a mission statement. Ken assisted in enabling in the development of a mission statement consistent with the owner's vision.

The Kohler family vision for Kohler Company was cast long before the current chairman, Herbert V. Kohler, Jr., was born. He did not divert the company from the vision of his ancestors; he refined and expanded it. Under his leadership, the company continued to grow as a nationally-recognized manufacturer of plumbing fixtures and fittings, engines and generators. Herb expanded the company's real estate development and its small hotel, the American Club, into a large, successful hospitality division which now includes world-class golf courses. It was Herb's creative leadership and implementation of a focused mission statement that enabled the ongoing and unparalleled success of Kohler Company.

In 1975, the executives of Kohler met for five days to develop a mission statement and a long-range plan. The discipline for these meetings was "The Grid," a system developed by Blake and Mouton of Austin, Texas. The six executives meeting at the session were Herb Kohler, Sam Davis, John Lillesand, William Hatten, Walter Neverovich, and Ken Benson.

The words "gracious living" became the most important two words generated from these intense meetings and remain, to this day, the core of

Kohler Company's philosophy. Do the products and services of Kohler Company contribute to gracious living?

During this lengthy five-day planning session, each day's work began early in the morning and ended late in the evening. The executives candidly examined in depth both the Kohler Company operations as they actually were in 1975 and how they would be if they were ideal. The next step was to develop specific plans to reach the ideal. Each executive was expected to candidly share his thoughts on how they could all work effectively together, capitalizing on company strengths and eliminating its weaknesses.

The discussions were often intense and at times extremely personal. Ken particularly remembers being asked the one question that made him face up to his own vision of life. He was asked, "Just what are your priorities?"

After several moments of silence, Ken responded by saying, "My job at Kohler is my number three priority. My family is number two. My God is number one." He then quoted the Summary of the Law taught by Christ: "You shall love the Lord your God with all your heart, with all your soul, and with all your mind. This is the first and great commandment. And the second is like it. You shall love your neighbor as yourself."

The room remained silent for sometime and there was no further comment about Ken's priorities.

"Gracious living" continues to be the most important two words of Kohler Company's mission statement.

Your mission statement should represent the approach you intend to follow to make your vision a reality. In its simplest form, it could be adopted by other organizations that try to live and work with principles identical to your own. It will provide you with the guidelines you must follow to produce a reputable company which is always trying to be above reproach.

Actually, your service or product is not critical in this statement. What is critical is your integrity in living and working within its parameters. Al has always felt comfortable with Grube Pharmacy's mission statement:

"We are a Model of Quality and Service, Treating our Customers and Associates as Friends."

This statement is a challenge to practice on a daily basis, but the stronger your adherence to it, the more dedicated your customers will be because they have become your friends.

The Customer

by Ken Benson, President and Chief Operating Officer,
in the Vollrath Company monthly newsletter, V.I.P.

The Vollrath Company has an organization chart that shows who reports to whom. The top square on the chart is Terry Kohler, our Chairman and C.E.O. All the other various positions within the company follow. Mike Arbutina, Eastern Regional Manager of our Food Service Division, recently sent me a letter suggesting that we add a new square at the very top of the chart labeled "Customer." You're right, Mike. Without customers, none of us would have a job.

No matter what our job, we need to keep both the person who buys and uses our products in mind. Whether it is the quality of the product we are making, the promptness of our delivery, the planning of new products or the way we sell our products . . . the customer is truly our boss (and Terry's!). It is up to us to do such a good job that we profitably sell our products. This will permit us to grow and serve our customers better in the future. We'll change the organization charts as you requested, Mike! Here is the first edition:

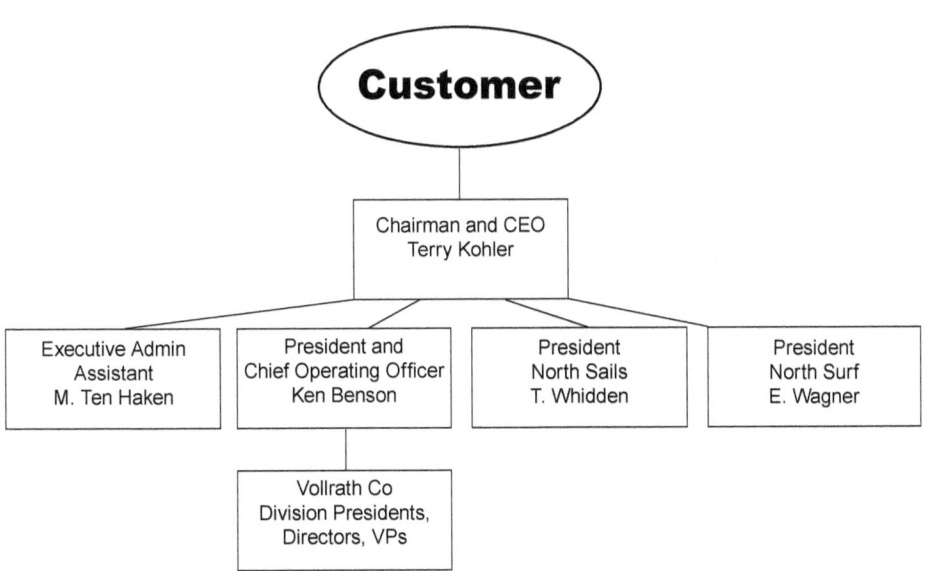

3. Candor in Communication

Candor in communication is truthful and uncomplicated information that is easily understood by the recipient.

Communication

Communication is the transfer of information from the purveyor to the recipient in a form the recipient can assimilate. The purveyor must make every effort to understand each recipient's preferred method of learning. Some are auditory learners. They find the spoken word or sound itself the easiest way to understand information.

Visual learners prefer to get information in the printed or written form. Even more meaningful can be pictures or illustrations of the information. "Can I see it?" is a typical visual learner's request. Undoubtedly, the statement, "a picture is worth 1,000 words," was spoken by a visual person.

The more sensual person is the kinesthetic learner. Without the ability to touch or feel the information, the information has little meaning to a kinesthetic. A hands-on person certainly is a kinesthetic individual.

Most of us learn in all three ways–auditory, visual, and kinesthetic–but in varying degrees. One way may predominate and that is the easiest way for the individual to learn.

It is important to gain your associates attention before communicating information that you wish your associates to understand. That is why it is imperative that you use the knowledge previously acquired about your associate's interests and skills. Your goal is to frame the information with subjects that are of interest to your listeners. Move from the associates interests and current knowledge to the new information that could be complex or unfamiliar. Learning is expedited by going from the known, from personal interests, to the unknown, where interest may be lacking.

You must continually review in your mind, "what do I know about my associates' family, or their interest in sports, their personal background, education, skills, and hobbies?" The more you know about them, the easier it is to communicate in a way they will understand. Bear in mind that each presentation increases retention and it stimulates interest. Call it "buying in."

Since many of us learn different skills by experiencing knowledge in different ways, it can be very useful to expose the associate to the same piece of information in different ways. It was an old rule that to teach an associate to have a complete understanding of the message, the same material must be communicated seven times in seven different ways. That increases retention.

There is no doubt that repetition is an important and valuable tool. Some learn a new skill quickly and forget it with the same speed. Repetition aids retention, but only if presented in different ways. Tuning out that which is boring is common in every social interaction. We all want our information to be fresh and exciting. The great communicators of our time try to keep their information fresh, keep it exciting, and vary how information is presented.

Your listener has many distractions to prevent the absorption of your message. Be ever conscious that you are competing for their undivided attention all of the time.

Many errors are based on the misunderstanding of the communication at hand. Frequently, the cost of correcting the error is both time-consuming and expensive. But probably even more critical is the impact on the associates' psyche and their willingness to do the task correctly the next time.

Not only must you be aware of your communicant's preferred learning style, but you must be aware of the limitations in their vocabulary skills. Using unfamiliar words will either draw blanks or cause the associate to misinterpret the information. While one may be able to judge the extensiveness of a person's vocabulary by being aware of their education level, the best approach is to listen carefully to the vocabulary the associate uses.

Always remember that communication only occurs when the speaker or communicator and the recipient understand each other. Without understanding nothing is accomplished, both parties become irritated, and future dialog becomes an exercise in futility.

The concept of informing the associate seven times in seven different ways might seem laborious and a waste of time. The goal is not to belittle or irritate the receiver, but rather to increase their interest in and retention of information you want them to have.

Candor

Candor seems like such an obvious word. "Mean what you say, and say what you mean," describes the responsibility of the communicator. What you are after is communication that permits mutual understanding. Take all of the buzzwords out of communication. Forget about spin, image, take, perception or whatever other fancy elusive words that might describe less than open, truthfulness. Any message should be candidly communicated.

For example, suppose President Nixon had appeared on television the day after the Watergate break-in and said, "My fellow Americans, last night some misguided subordinates of mine broke into the Democratic Headquarters at Watergate and stole information from their files. This happened on my watch and I take full responsibility for this reprehensible, illegal act. I have discharged all those who were in any way connected with the incident. I will candidly answer any questions that you might have. Any criminal actions commenced will be fully disclosed as the facts of this case unfold. I apologize for not being on top of this situation. I will make sure it doesn't happen again. Thank you and good night."

This candid disclosure would still set off a firestorm in the press. Certainly there would be congressional hearings and political outrage. But if President Nixon candidly disclosed events as he knew them, without giving thought to spin, he might well have served a full second term.

Instead, he lied to his wife, his family, his staff, congress and the American public. His recorded conversations that were eventually played back, revealed the sorry truth of what might otherwise have been characterized as an amateurish episode. The rest is history.

Candor, though important, will not clear up cloudy and vague communications.

A recent article in the Milwaukee Journal-Sentinel summarized a bill passed by the Wisconsin Legislature concerning the settlement of homeowner-contractor disputes. Homeowners would be required to give contractors one last chance, in writing, to remedy matters before suing them.

Sponsors of the bill said it was, "a way to solve building problems without running to court, although a person can eventually do that," and "if we can get everyone talking, we can stop small problems from becoming big ones."

Matt Moroney, executive director of the Metropolitan Builders Association of Greater Milwaukee said: "We see communication problems all the time. We tell the customer, 'Send a letter to your builder, detailing you concerns and send a copy to us.' That resolves 80 to 85 percent of all the disputes."

A clear, concise written contract, simply describing the work to be done by the contractor, would be a good starting point in the communications.

An honest intent by the contractor to effectively do the work and complete it as promised would be the next step. A good faith effort by the homeowner to work with the contractor without overreaching or hindering performance would enhance the climate for mutual trust. A candid and timely revelation of any problems that might arise between homeowner and contractor as the work progresses would lessen the likelihood of dispute.

Once a lawsuit is threatened by either party, the likelihood of open communications is lessened. Both parties are now on guard; their main goal becomes winning a lawsuit rather than having a candid discussion to solve a problem. Getting everyone to talk may stop small problems from becoming big ones, but getting everyone to listen is far more important. People tend to get defensive if all they do is talk.

Sensible Policies

At Mary Lee's Hallmark, a policy was established to pay a bonus of 5 per cent for all products that sold for more than $35. For example, a $50 item would net the employee who made the sale an extra $2.50. This would appear on a separate check, given once each month. The name for this bonus is "PM," for Percentage Merchandise. The associate had to participate in the sale. No bonus was given if a customer made the selection on his or her own, or was assisted by a new associate who was not yet eligible to earn the bonus. The associates were made aware that bonuses were given when they directly participated in making the sale, not for just ringing up the customer's purchase. This is an example of candor in communication.

Another example of candor practiced at Mary Lee's was this: if an associate does not want to work on a given day, he or she must find a replacement. Associates are told this when they accept the position. It is no problem; just find your replacement. The policy worked well and a lot of management time was saved.

For 44 years and thousands of deliveries, not one violation of established laws governing speed, recklessness or inconsiderate actions were ever called to Al's attention. It is assumed that the repetitious statement, "No delivery, no workload, no time frame takes precedence over considerate, careful, and safe driving" helped the drivers to achieve such a record. Luck played a factor, probably, but there were times Al had three vehicles on the road, as much at ten hours a day and sometimes seven days a week.

Al's nursing home pharmaceutical practice was a continuous and ongoing challenge. Because the homes were under constant scrutiny by the state, clients were assured that any challenges by state inspectors regarding the nursing home practices would be dealt with immediately in person by the division leader. Over the more than 20 years of service, the rule violations could easily be counted on one hand. They became minor challenges rather than serious charges. This is a statement that Al's colleagues in the area could not make.

Of course, Al's division leader was noted for his candor in communicating with the state inspectors.

In face to face communication we use all of our senses. We look people in the eye or don't. We move about rigidly, nervously, confidently or relaxedly while we are talking or listening. We send subtle signals of approval or disapproval by our word choice, tone of voice, body language and listening skills. We are in total communication regardless of whether our message is hostile, defiant, benevolent, gentle, condescending, passive, aggressive, loving, hateful, prejudiced, obtuse, angry or open and candid. A solution to a dispute is likely possible if both parties are willing to listen to each other, even giving themselves time to silently think a bit before responding to an idea that might seem contrary to their own perception of the problem.

Silence is a powerful tool of communication. Taking time to respond intelligently is far more impressive than a quick shot from the hip. Giving a person plenty of time to answer a question is more powerful than interrupting yourself to give the answer to your own question. Silence is eloquent and most important in all communication.

Candid communication is not trying to make everyone feel good about themselves. It is the honest effort to be understood about what you really mean to say and trying to seek the same understanding of any communication you receive. If both parties truly understand one another a lawsuit won't be needed to solve a problem. It is also possible that the mutual trust generated by candid communication will result in further successful transactions.

Candor will greatly assist your associate in performing their responsibilities effectively. You have opened the channels of effective communication by presenting the information in the easiest way your associate can absorb it. You have put the information in the context of their experience, repeated it seven times and in seven different ways, and have done so in words that are part of their vocabulary. Furthermore, you have done your very best to consider their communication preferences, be it auditory, visual, or kinesthetic. You have communicated with candor!

4. Trust

*__Trust__ is developed when honesty and integrity are openly
and consistently demonstrated throughout your organization.*

Trust is the ultimate goal of any leader. Once trust is established, a smooth running organization is a given. Without trust you are doomed to fail. Every organization will be underperforming if it does not have the supportive foundation of trustworthiness.

Trust means you can believe what your boss says. It means you can believe your subordinates are telling the truth. It means you can believe your peers and it means people are unafraid of being stabbed in the back or being the victim of vicious gossip.

Trust means that the financial condition of the company is openly and fairly represented to everyone in the company. It means people are not given a snow job to conceal bad news. It means what is represented about the company is truthful. It means that there is an umbrella of truthfulness covering everyone and that everyone is expected to candidly tell the truth.

If trust is absent in an organization, firewalls are built to protect management as well as the company. Rules are then established, monitored, and a system implemented for "breakers" of those rules. The cost in time, effort, and ill-will will consume profit.

Trust eliminates or greatly reduces the cost of monitoring. It encourages mutual respect and cooperation. Everyone working toward a common goal will assure a good measure of success.

We believe that people of integrity will consistently perform their jobs. Errors may occur, but a person making an honest mistake is free of any intent to create problems or willfully perform below expectations.

Trust starts at the top. Leaders, working within a trustful environment will by their own example set the tone. If a leader is fair, reasonable, considerate and consistent, subordinates are also more likely follow the same pattern. Consistently demonstrating trust and confidence in subordinates generates the same quality in them as they earn trust and prove their dependability.

A holistic environment of trust within your organization will be felt and understood by the customers. You must trust your associates and your providers of goods and services and they must trust you. Ultimately, your trustworthiness will rub off on your total environment, which includes your community, city, state, country, and, of course, your world.

Pictorially, this simple diagram epitomizes this statement:

Circle of Trust

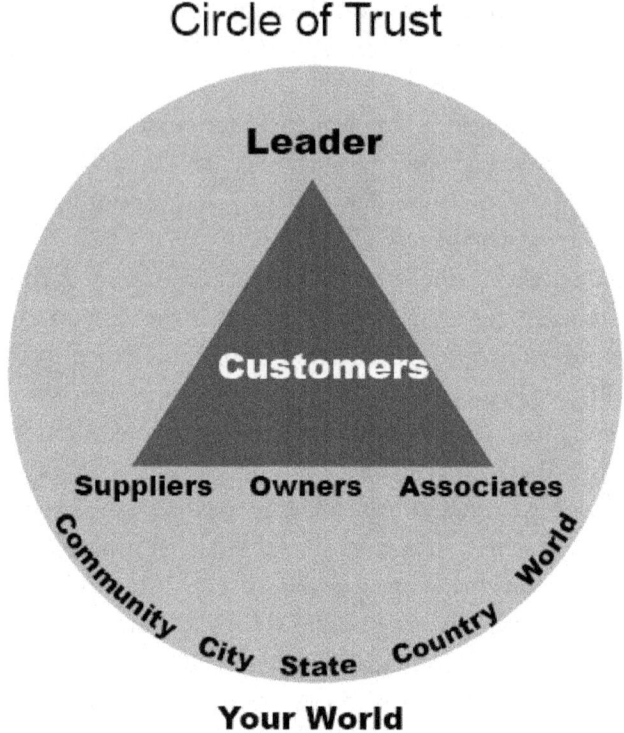

Your World

Trust must be mutual, between the owners, the leader, and the associates. It is essential that leadership set the tone, make the initial overtures, practice trust creation, and maintain it without fail on a consistent, daily basis.

Trust matures when people consider themselves friends and important to the success of the enterprise. Leaders should know their associates names, backgrounds, families, and interests. Everyone wants to feel important.

Once you trust the associate's abilities to perform and the associate trusts your decision-making skills, mistakes will only be what they really are—mistakes. The odious "intent" will never raise its ugly head and you can easily forgive and forget or correct the error.

Trust, like building a brick wall, is done one brick at a time. Begin building trust in the initial training period for each associate. As we said in the previous chapter, information must be easy to assimilate and must be communicated in the language, style, and tempo that the student can digest. Since each associate is different, a sincere effort must be put forward by the teacher-leader to accommodate the learner. This effort is an important part of the foundation of trust. Once you develop the skill to communicate with each individual the process becomes easy and fun.

What sorts of things should you, as the leader, explore to get to know a new associate?

Personal relationships are usually important to a new subordinate. Family is an easy place to start; parents, mates, children, and friends as well as interests such as hobbies, sports, and favorite ways to have fun. Asking about their goals is a more subtle way to find out about their hopes and dreams.

Some leaders may think that the effort to get to know their associates will take too much time, especially when it is suggested they record in writing what they learn. Yet most leaders have a difficult time remembering the minutiae about even a few of their direct subordinates. We think the time spent on this activity is a worthwhile investment in building trust.

Al's Trust

Al used an approach in his retail establishment that produced a good response and was easy to implement. It also provided its own governor to assure the task was completed. Upon hiring, Al gave each associate a copy of the booklet, "What's In It For You?" Its purpose was to explain what rewards the associate could expect for good performance and what the company expected from each associate.

Al recalls that some of his attempts to build trust were successful and others were not. Two of his successes helped create loyal employees who worked many years for Grube Pharmacy.

To insure that his business had someone capable of taking over should Al succumb to the uncertainties of life or death, he sold an interest in his company to a senior associate, Phil Mersberger. Al made an interest-free loan to Phil which was used to buy stock in Grube Pharmacy. Phil used earnings from Grube Pharmacy's profit-sharing plan to pay the principle on the loan. Of course, Al had to devise a bonus system related to a realistic measurement of his company's profit and of Phil's contribution to it.

Trust was established and maintained by having Grube Pharmacy's accounting firm review the biannual statement with the Phil, in a private session in which Phil was encouraged to ask any questions he might have.

Phil's profit-sharing bonuses enabled the loan to be paid off in less than five years. Thereafter, his share of the business profit was reinvested throughout his working career. When the business was sold, Phil had a nice nest egg to use as he desired.

This bonus plan created an attitude of trust and, more importantly, motivated the associate to do all within his power to make it a more successful enterprise.

Here is another one of Al's examples of trust: Al's in-house bookkeeper suggested that she might be leaving his employ within a year or two because of her husband's declining health. Jan Belitz was Al's delivery girl and had no experience or training in bookkeeping. She asked Al if she might be considered for the job when it became open. She asked Al if she could take time off to attend Lakeshore Technical College to study a two-year accounting course while working part-time for Al.

Al told Jan that he would arrange for her to work for him part-time and would also pay for her tuition and books if she would agree to work for him at least two years after completing the course. Jan was offered the opportunity to select her own work schedule while pursuing her studies. Al was surprised when Jan decided to work forty hours a week while attending Lakeshore Tech, the same number of hours she had worked before starting her education. She faithfully followed this strenuous schedule during her two years of study.

Jan graduated wearing the golden tassel at her class graduation ceremony. She was number one among her forty-five fellow classmates!

Al trusted Jan and he told her so. He had faith in her ability to do the job. Jan worked for Al as his in-house accountant for more than twenty-five years. You could say he was foolish for doing what he did, but Jan worked for Al until the day he retired. She continued to serve him for two more years as interim bookkeeper for Al and Mary's card and gift store. Jan saved Al large sums in outside accounting fees and Jan had challenging, rewarding and stable employment throughout her career.

Al trusted Jan and Jan trusted Al. Laugh if you will, but if this is foolishness, Al hopes there will be more opportunities for him to try to be foolish again.

Ken's Trust

When Ken was Vice President and General Counsel of Kohler Company, he was asked to inform the Wheel Horse Company, a garden tractor and snowmobile manufacturer, that Kohler would sue them unless they paid their delinquent account in full.

It was a cold winter day as the Kohler jet landed in South Bend, Indiana. Ken and Jack Myer, Kohler's Credit Manager, flew in to see what could be done to resurrect the Wheel Horse Company from sudden death.

Jack and Ken entered the gloomy, vacant administrative office of Wheel Horse which was adjacent to the quiet, lonely, spacious, dirty factory; it was completely shut down. Two lonely staff women occupied the otherwise empty office. Wheel Horse looked like a dead business. This once proud manufacturer of garden tractors, lawn mowers and snowmobiles had hit the skids. It couldn't pay its bills. No one would extend it credit. The CEO was in the hospital with a nervous breakdown; everything looked hopeless. Wheel Horse owed Kohler $350,000 and there didn't seem to be any likelihood of ever being paid unless the factory was running once again.

Jack and Ken noticed a large stack of snowmobile frames without engines on the factory floor. A factor official was roaming about the premises. A factor makes loans to a company using that company's inventory as collateral. The loan is repaid upon the sale of its products. Jack suggested that he and Ken talk things over with the factor official to see if something could be worked out. They proposed a plan where Kohler would sell engines to Wheel Horse using the factor's warehouse receipts as collateral. His response was positive.

Ken called Herb Kohler and asked for authority to extend Wheel Horse a $250,000 line of credit, secured by warehouse receipts, to purchase Kohler two-cycle snowmobile engines. Herb said, "You gotta be kidding. Why would we add $250,000 of credit to an unpaid debt of $350,000?"

Ken explained that the picture might come into better focus if Herb considered the fact that Kohler had an excess inventory of two-cycle snowmobile engines in its Canadian factory and many might have to be written off if left in stock. Ken told Herb that Jack and he saw the possibility of getting the Wheel Horse factory rolling if Wheel Horse purchased the engines to mount on its large stock of snowmobile frames. Wouldn't it be better to take the relatively low risk of shipping Wheel Horse two cycle engines that Kohler Company wasn't selling anyway to serve as a catalyst for Kohler to collect $600,000? Herb said that Ken would have to guarantee him that this scheme would work. Ken declined to do so, but added, that in his best business judgment, this plan had a good chance of working. Herb gave Ken his OK.

Kohler Company extended Wheel Horse credit and shipped $250,000 worth of two-cycle engines secured by the factor's warehouse receipts. Later, after returning to Kohler, Ken received a phone call from Twin Disc, a key Wheel Horse supplier of other snowmobile parts. The Twin Disc caller asked Ken what Kohler planned to do about its Wheel Horse account. Ken replied, "We've just extended them another $250,000 line of credit." Based on this information, Twin Disc expanded it's line of credit to Wheel Horse and continued to supply the key component snowmobile parts, thus enabling the manufacture of snowmobiles once again.

Once more, the Wheel Horse factory was humming with activity. Its employees were back on the job. Wheel Horse shipped snowmobiles to its customers.

Within a few months, Kohler Co. received $600,000 from Wheel Horse in payment of its account. Herb Kohler sent Ken a hand written note which read "You're entitled to twenty martinis!" Ken didn't drink on the job.

Some years later, Wheel Horse sold the company to AMC for several million dollars. This creative solution demonstrates the value of trust. Jack and Ken trusted each other; Herb Kohler trusted them; Ken and Jack trusted the factor; Twin Disc trusted Kohler Co.; all trusted Wheel Horse. Everyone was willing to take some risk.

Trust, like friendship, is built one step at a time. The leader must set the tone. The primary focus is to know each subordinate, not just name and responsibilities, but to know them as friends. Once you care about them you will be fair, consistent, and reasonable. You will have built the foundation of trust that will exist throughout your working life together.

5. Commitment

Commitment is the positive, continuous drive, energy and stamina required to accomplish the goal.

Clarifying your vision, establishing a mission statement, developing trust, and communicating with all the intensity and candor you can muster requires a strong commitment to make it all happen.

Once you have done all that, isn't it obvious you have made a commitment? Many make an early commitment, but once obstacles are encountered, vision and mission are re-thought and excuses are found to throw in the towel. This is not commitment; it is wishful thinking. We have not steeled ourselves against the many obstacles that will appear in our pathway to success and accomplishment.

This then becomes your mantra; your dream or vision leaves no room for your inner critic, the side of you that analyzes, creates excuses for failure, and moves the goal to the unattainable. You must adopt the mind set of a performer–Just Do It. Regardless of the obstacles or distractions, you just DO IT. You must convince yourself that you can and will DO IT! Failure is never considered. Your progress may be impeded, but never stopped. The journey of a thousand miles begins with the first step. Take one step at a time, each step independent of the others, until one day you have fulfilled your vision.

There is nothing more satisfying than participating in a project where everyone is truly committed to its success and then actually achieving it. A team that experiences this level of success is likely to repeat its success in other endeavors.

Management teams often spend several intense days in some far-off secluded place attempting to figure out who they are, what they are all about, where they are going and what they are going to do. This collegial atmosphere of struggling together for an extended period of time to define its mission statement and become committed to it serves as a bond for the group. Once each and every member of the team truly buys into the mission statement that they have poetically honed together, their commitment should be firmly in place.

To the outsider, the work product of a team in defining its mission statement may seem simplistic, mundane or even Pollyanish. "It's nothing more than God, country, motherhood, and apple pie" could be the comment of the outsider. But this kind of superficial treatment of their work would be insulting to the team members who have developed a full sense of mutual understanding what they are about and where they are going.

It is likely that a company will have a long run of success if all of its employees understand the mission statement and have also made a commitment to it through similar meetings.

The cracks in this happy portrayal begin when management and employees get sloppy about keeping on track. New employees and new members of the management team become suspicious of the acronyms and ill-defined lexicon that smacks of a secret society of the uninitiated. They feel left out or believe that only lip service is being given to the mission statement. Top management may have long since forgotten their commitment and those employees still hanging on conclude that it is all a superficial and meaningless charade.

Changing the Dynamics

Change in a small community is a slow process. But Al didn't have time to wait when he opened his first drugstore in 1955. He needed to do all within his power to win customers or his economic demise would be both quick and final.

Al decided to set store hours of 9 a.m. to 9 p.m., seven days a week, Sundays and holidays included. His competitors were open 10 a.m. to 6 p.m. Monday through Saturday and closed on Sundays and holidays. Al was not popular with his colleagues. If they wanted to compete, they were forced to change. But they dawdled long enough to let Al get a foothold.

Grube Pharmacy added free delivery regardless of the cost of the order. It was prompt, the drivers were considerate, and prices were competitive. Pharmacists took calls when the store was closed between 9 p.m. and 9 a.m., which offered the customer 24-hour service. Few customers used the overnight ordering service, but the public relations value was helpful.

Every idea he had didn't work, of course, but enough of them did so that Grube's sales volume was consistently greater than the big-name chains that came to the Sheboygan area after Grube Pharmacy was established.

Al found himself running a successful drugstore and desired to expand. But expansion presented some challenges. It seemed to require large investments. A shortage of pharmacists was appearing on the horizon and growth appeared quite far off in the future. Was there a faster route to economic success?

The nursing home industry was becoming an attractive alternative. A friend of one of Al's associates was building Morningside Nursing Home, a new 72-bed facility. It provided Al with an opportunity. Al convinced the developer that an exclusive pharmacy provider would benefit his facility. Al rented a small space within Morningside and developed a system he called "daily dose dispensing." Al would package the meds for each nursing home resident, a task then performed by the nursing staff. Nurses would then simply administer the drugs. This saved huge amounts of nursing time, reduced medication errors, and saved the patients money because discontinued meds were never billed. It was a win-win situation.

The advantages to the nursing home and its patients were obvious, but Al discovered that offering the services to nursing homes in-house with a pharmacy staff present for four hours each day was not economically practical. So he increased the work load of the nursing home pharmacy by developing a senior citizen discount prescription program. Any senior, not just those living in Morningside, could come in to have prescriptions filled. The program was promoted through the senior center and to local unions for their retired members. This innovation brought in new customers made the Morningside operation profitable.

Since the idea was unique, Al wrote an article about it which was printed in a pharmaceutical journal. A year later someone else using the concept developed the "unit dose program," which involved sealing each dose of medication independently in its own plastic envelope. This enhancement allowed Al to win the exclusive business of preparing prescription drug doses for residents of many of the nursing homes in the area. This business grew to serve 1,200 beds and took in annual revenue of almost $2.5 million.

Al's business remained local, but had his vision been exported, it could have grown much larger. Al sold the nursing home division in 2001 as he neared retirement, and today the national company he sold it to serves at least 100,000 nursing home beds. A point well taken: The size of your vision affects the size of its outcome.

Al's floor space grew

Grube Pharmacy started with 5,000 square feet and grew to about 10,000. By today's standard, that is small potatoes. But at the time, it was the largest independent in the city and about the same size as chain competitors. Today 20,000 to 30,000 square feet is common and some drugstores are even larger.

The added space was quickly absorbed by non-drug products. Once the chains decided to continue to grow in floor space, Grube's was out of the growth competition.

"I was happy I was able to be an independent pharmacy," Al said, "but even I had growing pains. Maybe one could say I was part of an era which has moved on."

A costly lawsuit

Ken spent the better part of eight years at Kohler Company working with Lu Chase on a complex antitrust case. The entire plumbing ware industry was charged with price-fixing. Criminal charges were brought against many key executives. Class-action triple-damage civil suits were filed against the industry by homeowners, plumbing contractors, plumbing distributors, federal, state and local governments. In other words, practically everyone in the country was suing the industry. What could cause such a mess?

It all began in the early 1960's with a dishonest executive director of the Plumbing Fixture Manufacturers Association, a trade organization intended to enhance both the image and practices of the industry. But this conniving executive director recorded numerous phone conversations with industry executives, enticing them to discuss prices and other practices that were clearly illegal under the Sherman Antitrust Act. In 1963, he embezzled more than $200,000 from the trade association, bought a yacht and sailed to the Bahamas with his family.

The shocked industry executives who served on the board of directors of the trade association hurriedly met and decided to turn the case over to the authorities. They were informed by the executive director that if they turned him in, he would turn all of his phone tapes over to the criminal antitrust division of the Justice Department in Washington D.C. The executives were outraged by this blackmail threat and reported the theft to the authorities. The executive director was arrested. He turned thirty-two tape recorded phone conversations over to the Justice Department and worked out a plea bargain with the authorities. He spent the next six months in a comfortable jail near Washington D.C. assisting the antitrust division develop its case against the plumbing manufacturing industry and its executives. Criminal charges were brought against several industry executives and the companies.

The jury trial was held in Federal District Court in Pittsburgh. It began in January, 1969, and was concluded in mid-May of the same year. After five hours of deliberation, the jury found the executives guilty as charged. Many of the executives paid large fines and served 30 to 90 days in jail.

Ninety-one class action civil suits were then started nationwide. These cases were consolidated into one huge case to be heard in the Federal District Court in Philadelphia. More than one hundred lawyers packed the courtroom at these early pre-trial hearings of this massive class action. At times, the courtroom was overflowing with lawyers.

Since there had been convictions in the criminal case, wrong-doing had already been established. Only monetary damages had to be proved to make a plaintiff eligible for an award three times the amount of the actual damage. Although it did not seem that damages could easily be proved by any of the plaintiffs, the global magnitude and legal consequences of ninety-one class actions hanging over the heads of the plumbing companies persuaded the industry executives to seek a global settlement with all parties to end, once and for all, these potential liabilities.

Finally, the companies worked out a settlement proposal by first contributing more than $20 million under a sharing agreement as a settlement pool. After negotiating a settlement with all the plaintiffs' lawyers, notice of the settlement proposal was mailed by the thousands to potential claimants. The settlement proposal was published nationally, including a full-page notice in the Reader's Digest in the hope that its 17 million readers might respond if they had a claim. The contingent lawyers fees of $5 million were deducted from the $20 million pool and the balance was dispersed to the claimants after the filing deadlines had passed.

How is this event related to commitment? The mission of enhancing the plumbing industry by establishing a trade association to help improve product and educate the consumer seemed like a noble idea. Yet the commitment of the association's executive director was not there. His goal was to embezzle the association's funds. The industry executives on the association board of directors were misguided and naive. They did not seem to fully understand how to conduct business in full compliance with antitrust laws. They did not comprehend the severe consequences of violation of these laws. Many had some prior training in this area and had been warned of the consequences of violating the law. Nevertheless, they failed to comprehend that the persuasive and subtle recorded phone conversations with the trade association executive director were leading them into a trap that crossed the threshold into a violation of the price-fixing laws.

Millions of dollars were spent defending the companies and its executives. Thousands of hours were consumed in extracting a whole industry from a hopeless mess. Executives who served their time in prison would never be the same. Years after the event, annual compliance reports were regularly filed by the companies with the court. Think of the value the plumbing industry might have enjoyed had everyone been clearly committed to the association's simple mission of improving their products and educating the consumer. Think what might have happened if the millions of dollars, energy, time and hard work consumed by each company in defending and settling these cases could have been directed toward the profitable marketing of improved products.

An entrepreneur must persist in being fully committed to his vision. But the commitment is a two-way street. It cannot prevail without the total commitment to the mission statement of all the associates in the business. Committed employees may fulfill your vision if you are truly committed. There can be no double standard. You must truly and consistently maintain and earn the trust of your associates, demonstrating to them that you are fully committed to both your business and those who work for you. Hard productive work, trust and a clear understanding of the mission of your business will help earn this lasting commitment of your associates. Commitment will be reciprocal.

From your vision you will develop a mission statement with the participation of associates eager to make it happen. If the direction is clear, your excitement and enthusiasm will encourage them to participate.

Then everyone can truly say "We have made a commitment."

Join the 3-H Club

by Ken Benson

in 'Let's Talk', the Vollrath Company's newsletter

 In the November 16 issue of the "Industry Week," the editorial written by Perry Pascarella is entitled, "3-H Club Undermines Corporate Mediocrity." He writes about Hustle, Humility and Humor in the workplace. These three words appeal to me, notwithstanding my youthful indoctrination as a 4-H member to pledge my head, heart, hands, and health.

No doubt about it, there is a hustle to business if we are to maintain that sense of urgency to do a job both well and on-time. But hustle is different than frantic scurrying. This is where humility comes in. We all need to be willing to pitch in when a job needs doing.

All of this can seem grim unless we maintain our sense of humor. Our work should be fun. There is no reason why we can't work safely and productively and still have fun. We need to maintain a spirit of both joy and success. While we hustle, we need to be willing to help the person next to us and have fun. I like these three H's so I guess I'll add them to the four I learned in my youth.

6. Spirit

***Spirit** is the energy and enthusiasm that keeps one moving forward.*

Any business worth its salt should be fun. Employees and executives should maintain a joyful spirit and feel motivated to do what they are doing because they like what they are doing. That's a tall order if a business is to stay on track, satisfy its customers, employees, stockholders and the public and at the same time maximize profits.

You can't fake fun. You can't paint a happy face and proclaim that everything is great when it really isn't. The spirit of a successful business must be genuine. Is there some sort of internal flywheel that generates its own energy for the next success? What is this thing called spirit? Is this perpetual motion? Not likely. Yet you can intuitively feel the pulse of the spirit of a business the moment you walk into it.

If everyone is grim-faced carrying a resigned look that says, "tell me what you want me to do, and I'll do it," you are looking at a troubled business. If the manager is complaining to his customers about the ineptness of his employees in the very presence of those employees, you have identified a sick business about to fail.

On the other hand, when employees pleasantly help each other without expecting something more or cheerfully go the extra mile to help a customer, you can feel the strength of these efforts; they likely will perpetuate further good works within the business. Even when something is boring it can be fun if everyone pitches in to accomplish the task.

Management can create an ambiance of good humor and good works by the way they present ideas, policy and tasks to their associates. Honesty, candor, trust and fair treatment are the underpinnings for all of this. Even when things seem grim, these underpinnings will carry you through the rough spots. Humor is especially important when things aren't working out. But it must be relevant and honest humor directed toward the problem and its solution. If we can laugh at our misfortunes and enjoy the satisfaction of mitigating or correcting them, we are on our way to more successes and a better spirit within our business.

It seems essential to talk about morale within an organization. Dissecting it into some of its components is not quite so simple. We wanted to consider it as spirit, but that wasn't complete enough. If we added humor, that broadened the base a bit, but for all of us to feel satisfied it seemed we needed to include hard work as well.

Obviously, we all would prefer productive, happy, and cooperative associates. Yet, who is probably responsible for most of the low morale? It almost always emanates from the leader, who, in most cases, was selected by a superior, not by the group being led. As mentioned in an earlier chapter, it is essential that the leader make every effort to get to know all his associates. The more that's known and shared, the more people see each other as friends they care about. In larger organizations the same need for understanding applies within the various departments, but is obviously not attainable among thousands of associates.

You must be available to answer questions, quick to acknowledge associates whenever they have done something extra. Be free to praise, and slow to blame. Remember a basic principle of management: praise in public, blame in private.

Encourage your associates to have fun, and to enjoy each other. Try to resolve conflicts as fairly and as quickly as possible. Consider both sides of an issue. Jumping to conclusions without knowing the facts and understanding both sides of an issue before making a decision can be destructive to a healthy and pleasant work climate.

Each of us has an ego that we don't want attacked. We all want to feel important, needed, and cared about. Think about how good you feel when someone sings your praises in the presence of others. Working hard is always easier to do when you are appreciated for your efforts.

Another cardinal rule of management is praise for performance; tell people when they do a good job. Also, take full responsibility when things aren't working well. Sincerity is obvious, so if you don't believe it, don't say it. An untruth is very destructive. This is the easiest way to build distrust.

Al found a useful tool to create some of the camaraderie in his drugstore. He brought every employee together for a monthly meeting. Once a month, except December and July, he held a meeting from 9:15 p.m. to 10:30 p.m. after the store closed for the day. It was mandatory; he took attendance and paid employees for their time. He got some complaints, but the only excuses accepted were vacation, sickness, or death. There were very few absences.

The meetings gave the staff from one shift the opportunity to meet those from another. New staff members were introduced and they talked about some of their interests. Al discussed policy changes and informed staffers of new product categories. Al had members of the staff open the meeting and lead their fellow workers in the store's Mission Statement "We are a Model of Quality and Service, Treating our Customers and Associates as Friends."

The meeting was also closed by a staff member who led the group in the company yell, "I make a difference!" In each

Al, dressed as a North High School cheerleader, leads the cheer, "I make a difference," at a staff meeting.

meeting, a pre-selected staff member told and showed pieces of new, or special stocked items, describing their sales features and making personal comments on how they planned to sell them.

Special events in staff members lives were recognized and refreshments served. Many times the staff members brought additional treats to recognize special events in their lives. The meetings followed a format so everyone knew ahead of time what was to be discussed. The assignments were rotated and announced at least one month before the meeting.

It is Al's belief that the more involved the staff are, the friendlier and the more cooperative they will be. Admittedly, every staffer's presentation wasn't perfect, but if nothing else happened, they became better sales people.

Ken's twenty-three year career with Kohler Company was a challenge to him. He both enjoyed the work, yet was often frustrated with it. He felt mired down in boring legal research, drafting reams of legal memos, reviewing volumes of fine print, memorializing and dating events for the files. He saw no end to the boredom of it all. To this day, he still experiences flashback dreams of this endless, monotonous, trivial, bureaucratic work that seemed to go nowhere. But he also had many exhilarating experiences.

He travelled to new places, enjoyed the discreet mentoring of Lucius Chase in all his brilliance, and met learned professionals of national notoriety. Ken eventually stepped out on his own and enjoyed the satisfaction of helping solve problems both within and outside the company.

In October 1959, Ken played the role of Drumond, the Clarence Darrow character in the Sheboygan Community Player's production of "Inherit the Wind." He immersed himself in this re-creation of the 1925 Scopes "monkey" trial regarding the challenge of teaching evolution in the classroom in Dayton, Tennessee. His portrayal of Drumond was his catharsis; it purged him of his frustrations at work. It gave him the courage and strength to type a letter to Herbert V. Kohler, Sr.

Ken was weary of hearing the self-serving, stereotypical political cliches flow from the lips of Kohler Company office employees and executives. He began to think that people moved their lips, spouting politically correct aphorisms before their brains were functioning. What better way to express his concerns than by personally typing a three-page letter to Herbert V. Kohler, Sr., the CEO? The letter contained Ken's candid review of what he thought were the company's strengths and weaknesses. He admitted that

In 1959, Ken played Drumond in "Inherit the Wind." This photo, signed by the playwrights, reads, "For Ken and all our friends at the Sheboygan Players—Warmly, Jerome Lawrence, Robert E. Lee.

one year's service with the company might be too brief for such candid observations. Notwithstanding these weaknesses, Ken handed his letter to Mr. Chase on February 2, 1960, the first anniversary of his employment, and asked to have it delivered to Mr. Kohler. Mr. Chase read the letter, smiled and made no comment. To this day, Ken does not know whether Mr. Chase ever delivered the letter.

It took fifteen years service in the legal department before Ken was liberated from the law and challenged to become an executive. In 1974 he was promoted to Senior Vice President of the company. His new office was on the fourth floor, adjacent to the boardroom and across the hall from the office of the new CEO, Herbert V. Kohler, Jr., the same office occupied by his father. There were only four offices on that top floor: for Herb, his secretary, Ken, and his secretary. When Ken began work in 1959, he took an oath to himself that he "would not have sweaty hands when he was called to fourth floor". Now he was there; his hands remained dry.

Ken's office was formerly occupied by Walter Cleveland, president of the company. Walter told Ken, some years after his retirement, that he was able to survive for five years in that office on the fourth floor. He implied that this was some kind of record. Ken lasted eight years in this same office before he resigned on January 31, 1982. His hands were getting sweaty.

You might ask Ken, why would he resign at age 52 in the middle of a recession when he seemed to be doing pretty well in life? Why would he decide to quit when he had no other job offer, four of his five children were in college, had a large mortgage on his home and could be in danger of losing everything by such a stupid move?

Two Kohlers

Ken has had the opportunity of working with both Herbert V. Kohler, Jr. and his second cousin, Terry Kohler. Herb and Terry are both talented businessmen. But they are complete opposites. This is the first time Ken has written about these differences and his personal experiences working with them.

Herb Kohler, Jr.

Herb was fifteen years old when Ken began his career at Kohler Company in 1959. One of Ken's first legal assignments was to draft a circus contract between Kohler Company and the Christiani Brothers Circus. This special event, scheduled for the summer of 1959, was for the enjoyment of all Kohler employees and their families. Sometime after the circus, Ken learned that Herb had participated in the tightrope act with Christiani circus tightrope walkers.

After Herb graduated from Yale, he tested his acting abilities at Knox College. He honed his manufacturing skills by apprenticing under Sam Davis, then plant manager of the Spartanburg, South Carolina, plant. He finally returned to the home office in Kohler as vice president of manufacturing. It was here that Ken had his first opportunity to work with Herb. Herb was then twenty-nine years old.

Herb has a joy for life that has always been one of his greatest assets. He truly loves what he does and participates with intensity and gusto. He has charisma and is fun to work with. His charm and curiosity promote an ambiance of creativity. He mandates the highest standard of quality in any pursuit undertaken by the Kohler Company.

Herb has excellent judgment and excels in strategic, creative thinking. He also has a good eye for design which is extremely helpful in product development, advertising and real estate planning.

But Herb can be a difficult boss. He can turn off that special quality of leadership that captures the imagination, allegiance, devotion and spirit. A loyal employee must sustain himself through these bad times by drawing from his reservoir of good spirits from past good works with Herb.

As the years passed, Ken perceived his spirit of joy and creativity being snuffed out. He knew he had outlived his usefulness and should leave Kohler Company, notwithstanding the many good years he experienced in his twenty-three year career. His decision came about gradually as he experienced an erosion of his working relationship with Herb. Clearly, if someone were to resign from Kohler Company, it would not be Herb.

Summarizing a few of these experiences best illustrates why Ken felt the time had arrived for him to leave. The late Lyman Conger, former Kohler Board Chairman and CEO, often quoted O.A. Kroos, an early Executive Vice President of the company who said, "The Kohler's have neither clocks nor calendars." Therein lies one of the potential spirit-killers.

Herb would often schedule a meeting for 10 a.m. that would not actually begin until 10 p.m. and then continue on into the wee hours of the morning. At 2 a.m. one morning, Ken recalls sitting at the large table in the board room in a private meeting with Herb as they contemplated the correct amount of white space between the "K" and the "O" on a KOHLER matchbook cover that was about to be printed. Herb understood the importance of disciplined and consistent corporate identity. So did Ken. But this seemed like overkill.

Herb could take equally long in reaching what seemed to Ken to be timely decisions. In Ken's eyes, a perfect decision made too late is worthless. Ken may have been too impetuous at times for Herb may well have had good reasons for his delays; but they were not revealed to Ken as he impatiently waited to get on with it.

Ken recalls the day that Bill Krekel, Vice president and chief financial officer of Kohler, nervously shuffled several stacks of the collated papers of a financial report which he was soon to present to Herb and the board. He asked Ken, "Should I use a paper clip or a staple on this report?" Ken thought this was a perfect illustration of how paralyzed one could get when fear blocks even the smallest decision.

Once the spirit of joy and fun of work is killed, angry frustration often replaces it. Ken felt thwarted, even worthless in his job. In his perception, he faced barriers that kept him from doing his job well. In his frustration, his own bluntness and outspokenness exacerbated the strained relationship he had with Herb. Hostility between two top executives in adjoining offices is not a climate for a creative and successful business. It was time to resign. Ken's spirit was broken, and Herb had lost confidence in Ken as well.

Terry Kohler

Terry Kohler was a casual acquaintance of Ken's for many years. It was only after Ken's defeat in the congressional primary election in February, 1959, that they became better acquainted.

Shortly after the election, Terry called Ken and asked to meet with him. Terry was running for the U.S. Senate. He discussed Ken's campaign experiences. Terry asked Ken if he would share his mailing lists, hoping to broaden his base of support in the forthcoming 1980 fall primary election. Ken shared his ideas and experiences with Terry and gave him the names and addresses of his key campaign supporters.

Several months later, a week before the election, Terry called Ken and invited him to lunch at Nino's restaurant. They had a pleasant lunchtime conversation. Then, Terry surprised him. He asked Ken if he would head up his Senate staff in Washington if Terry won the election. Ken was silent. At that time he hadn't even decided for whom he would vote. Ken told Terry he would like to think it over. He never responded; Terry lost the primary election the week following their meeting.

In October, 1981, Terry invited Ken to join him for lunch at River

Wildlife. Terry asked Ken whom he would recommend to fill a new executive position at Vollrath Company, Vice President of corporate Development. Ken made some recommendations.

Ken's forthcoming resignation from Kohler Company had not been made public, nor had there been any leaks of the resignation agreement he and Herb had negotiated. Ken knew at the time of his meeting with Terry that under the terms of his Kohler agreement, he would be resigning from Kohler Company some time between January 31 and April 1, 1982. The exact date would be determined by Herb, depending upon the successful opening of the American Club.

Ken talked with his good friend Gene Hodson about the possibility of joining the law firm of Hopp, Hodson and Powell. Gene told Ken that he believed something could be worked out, emphasizing that Ken would have to be his own rainmaker; no salary, no rewards. Everything would be based solely on the fees he generated.

Two weeks after his meeting with Terry, Ken called Terry and said, "I've thought about another candidate for your new position."

"Who?", Terry asked.

"Me," was Ken's response.

A few days later, Ken had a dinner meeting at Windway Capital Company with Terry, the CEO, and Chuck Andrews, President and Chief Operating Officer of the Vollrath Company, to discuss the new position and what Ken might have to offer. Some days later after Terry and Chuck had the opportunity to privately discuss the matter, Terry called Ken and offered him the job. Ken asked that he be elected to the Vollrath's board of directors and Terry agreed to recommend his election. Ken was to fill the new office of Vice President of Corporate Development and would be responsible for marketing, advertising, public affairs, legal, corporate planning, and international business.

Ken's first day of employment at Vollrath Company was April 1, 1982. Working for Terry Kohler was a completely new experience for Ken. Terry is a brilliant, impatient executive who delegates freely and wants people to do the job they were hired to do. He hates long, meaningless meetings. His bright mind races to conclusion "C" while everyone else is at "B." Furthermore, he wants to be on with it! This can be extremely intimidating to a young, insecure executive who desires to please more than to lead. The timid ones tended to chase off in whatever direction Terry's creative mind signaled. Unfortunately, the Vollrath Company had neither the resources nor the skills to attempt this many ventures. Ken's lack of fear served as a stabilizer in this climate and permitted a better focus on the business at hand.

But it was more than that. Ken and Terry were compatible. Terry could bluster without Ken flinching. Ken could shout back, yet both understood it was merely a vigorous exchange of ideas. Ken attempted to remain focused on only a few of Terry's creative ideas. Terry Kohler's exterior bluntness concealed his true character; he is a very generous and fair man, sensitive to the needs of his community. His employees trust him for they know he is an honest, caring, creative and demanding man. The spirit of the Vollrath Company was good and more fun-loving than that of the Kohler Company. But the business practices and capabilities of Vollrath were far less sophisticated than those of Kohler, even though Vollrath possessed one of the most advanced information systems in industry.

It was Terry's goal to decentralize Vollrath. His unorthodox solution was brilliant. In the fall of 1984, at a planning meeting of all the executives, Terry announced that everyone in the room was fired. Applications were open for executives to create and ask for any job they wanted within the company. But they were also expected to continue in their present positions until Terry decided what, if any, new job they might undertake with the company.

Ken promptly sent his job application to Terry. He stated that his first preference under the new order would be to serve as an independent consultant. His second choice was to be CEO of the company. Terry briskly walked into Ken's office and said, "Why if you were CEO, I wouldn't be able to make the decisions!" "You've got it!", Ken quickly replied. Terry urged Ken to stay on as Vice President of Corporate Development and watch over and nurture the whole decentralization process. Ken agreed to do so.

Some months later, Ken wrote Terry a letter stating that he believed he could more successfully work with Terry if he were President and Chief Operating Officer of the company, serving under Terry as CEO. He emphasized that if he had the opportunity to be president, he would always keep Terry fully informed, welcoming him to join any meetings he chose to attend. Terry did not immediately respond to his letter. Ken perceived some tension from Terry as he contemplated Ken's proposal. About two months later, in March, 1985, Ken was elected President of the company.

Total decentralization of Vollrath was completed by December 31, 1989, five years after Terry's goal was announced. By then, all corporate offices had been dissolved. Small independent businesses were organized to replace the former corporate structure. Key executives were offered the opportunity to buy stock in the new businesses they were to run.

Ken retired from Vollrath Company on December 31, 1989 and remained in a consulting capacity on an as-needed basis for three years thereafter. His years at Vollrath were some of the happiest years of his life. He and Terry remain good friends.

Spirit is the by-product of candor, trust, and commitment. These three vehicles in motion make the environment susceptible to fun. Because you are having fun, it is proof-positive that you are in a friendly environment where the participants know and like their fellow associates.

When you know your cohorts, you can laugh at or with them without any fear or concern of repercussions, you are free. In essence knowing and liking your associates serves as a catalyst to reach a common goal. That comfort zone of friendship certifies that spirit is present, providing an excellent climate for a successful and growing business.

Vollrath decentralizes
from the Vollrath Co. newsletter, V.I. P.

The achievement of a five-year goal—the decentralizing of The Vollrath Company—was announced today by Terry Kohler.

In conjunction with the realignment, Ken Benson, chief operating officer for the duration of this effort, announced his retirement from his full-time executive position as president of the company.

The former operating divisions are now completely separate corporations, with ownership control in Windway Capital Corporation, a holding company led by CEO Kohler and owned by his family.

"Ken Benson has been the game coach and quarterback over the transition period," Kohler said. "Through his five years of leadership, he has passed on his executive maturity, objectivity and clarity of vision to our younger generation management team. He has helped them become quality executives.

"It is time for Ken and me to stand aside . . . and let youth demonstrate how well we passed the baton," Kohler added. "We will both be around if they yell, but they are the superstars."

7. Monitor

Monitor means to review pertinent information to determine the success of your current operation, permitting timely change where needed.

Monitoring is a more formal way of understanding the strengths and weaknesses of yourself, your associates, your management practices and the operations within your organization. It is your responsibility not only to ask questions, but to openly seek ideas from your associates.

By developing an understanding of the business and how your people work together, you can capitalize on the strengths within your organization and mitigate its weaknesses. This is why we advocate getting to know yourself, the people within the business and the business itself.

Monitoring a course in college was to some a comfortable mechanism for attending the course without taking the final exam; no need to worry about a low grade; no fear of an entry on the transcript that might reduce the grade point. No credit, no risk. This is not what monitor means here. But, many students monitor a course to broaden their knowledge and to enhance their understanding of a subject. Learning is the goal, not the course credit.

The negative connotation of the word, monitor, is not what we advocate. We should monitor each other and ourselves, but not under a climate associated with spying, underhandedness and unfairness or "gotcha" techniques. This triggers the elimination of trust and destroys the spirit and harmony necessary for the long-term profitable success of a business.

We should monitor constructively, harvesting the mutual benefits resulting from the candid and relevant monitoring of each other. It should be with understanding and openness, free of threat of reprisals. Monitoring should seek and hopefully find solutions that improve the business and enhance the long-term careers of all associated with the business.

Monitoring should be done informally. Discussions should not be mechanically recorded. Summaries should be made afterwards and be available to all participants. A strategy for monitoring employees might involve answering these six questions:

1. Who are they?

It is critical that a leader understands the basics about the associates he is to monitor as well as how to respond when his associates monitor him. In other words, if you privately and gently inform your boss that he has bad breath, you would hope that he would thank you and use Listerine rather than fire you, put you on hold for a promotion, or cancel your next pay raise.

A leader should be comfortable using the first names or nicknames of associates in an informal way. Versatility in conversation with the associates includes talking about loved ones, their educational and training background, skills that could be useful in the work place, and different areas of their away-from-work life. If you can share their goals and desires, it can be helpful in explaining new procedures.

A periodic review of the monitor summaries, and some uninhibited chatter will enable a better understanding of the new associate. To put a time frame on this, within the first 90 days, a new associate should have ascended to the position of a new friend whose start button or attention stimulators are well-known.

2. Does everyone fit in?

Has the new associate been accepted by fellow associates? Was it a free and easy acceptance or did their new colleague have to push to become part of the team? While an individual's pace and productivity can vary from day to day, is the new person's output comparable to that of other associates?

The bottom line is that the new associate must be performing to a reasonable standard. In time, a new associate should indicate pride in the work being done.

Every interested and involved associate should be punctual. The associate's interest can be measured by how timely he or she is, and by the concern expressed when he or she is unexpectedly detained. Accepting responsibility for one's assignment is proof of the associate's interest and commitment.

By the end of six months, you should be convinced by monitoring your new associate that further effort is worth your time, that development will occur and a very valuable associate will have been found. If you are not convinced, your search for a replacement should begin.

3. Do associates accept your system, or should the system itself be changed?

Is the associate's progress in learning job responsibilities and performing them at a reasonable pace obvious, or are they totally dependent on their colleagues for support to complete their tasks?

Does he or she cooperate with associates and demonstrate a strong desire to be part of the team? By now their presence should be accepted and welcomed.

Other members of the team should be pleased with them and find them easy to work with. They should be willing to assist when they are having difficulties. A new associate should be willing to volunteer for more challenging assignments and be available to help others who may be having difficulties on a given project. Each associate should be versatile and be able to problem-solve.

It may take several years for a new associate to fully understand the job and reach the optimum level of performance. The time frame could be shorter, but two years appears the mean average for most associates. There is always the possibility that a new associate is very quick and perceptive; it may take less time for total integration in this case. It is a rare find to have such a person on your staff.

4. Do they demonstrate promotable skills?

Dedication to the job becomes obvious when you observe how an associate carries out responsibilities. They will show enthusiasm for their own projects. They will exhibit a sense of innovation, exploring different ways to accomplish the task. They will be open to new possibilities. Far too often, associates respond by rote. It is the same thing over and over.

The associate must be realistic about any changes suggested. Change is not practical just for change's sake. The leader must also be realistic and be capable of logical evaluation of the associate's proposal. Is the leader close-minded, or is he willing to listen to new ideas that permit change?

Promotability means that the associate is available to accept additional responsibility, and that he or she can easily adjust to the changes this will require. Here it is critical that the leader be familiar with the associate's personal life and other mitigating circumstances that might create problems that should be addressed before a decision is finalized.

5. Do I listen with understanding?

Listening is one of the most difficult skills for any executive or manager.

Good ideas are often squelched by an overpowering urge to interrupt.

6. Is there active, uninhibited participation in the monitoring process by associates?

Participation helps develop management skills in associates and helps keep the leader on the right track. Constructive criticism should be welcomed as a source of new ideas.

Use these six criteria in a logical sequence to monitor your associates and yourself. This will put you in a strong position to maximize the output of your associates and strengthen your leadership role.

Statistics and accounting data alone will not help you here. You may also need a simple narrative describing your goals. The accounting data and statistics will be helpful in measuring the bean-counting part of a profitable enterprise; the narrative measurement may help measure the soul of your vision.

Monitoring your business practices and operations is equally as important as monitoring the progress of your associates. Mutually monitoring each other is a necessity to successfully understand your business and where it can improve. If you are the leader of your business, your associates should have an ongoing opportunity to monitor you.

Al carried a 3 x 5 index card in a slot in his Daytimer, a calendar that

---

TRAINING PHILOSOPHY

1. We believe every employee wants to do a good job.

2. We believe learning occurs in different ways in different people.

3. We believe the approach to learning should be simple, repetitious, and inspiring.

4. We believe that only through ownership will employees permanently change their behavior.
   Ownership occurs by:
   a. Participation and Practicing
   b. Making Commitments
   c. Sharing Success
   d. Encouraging Others

MAGIC QUESTIONS TO ASK

What's being rewarded?

What should be rewarded?

OVER

REWARD FOR

1. Solid Solutions
2. Risk Takers
3. Creativity
4. Decisive Action
5. Smart Work
6. Work Simplification
7. Quietly Effective
8. Loyalty
9. Quality Work
10. Team Work

REWARDS

1. Money
2. Recognition
3. Time Off
4. Favorite Work
5. Advancement
6. Piece of the Action
7. Personal Growth
8. Freedom
9. Fun
10. Prizes

he carried to keep track of his planned events. The front of the index card listed the four keys to a training philosophy and the two "magic questions" to ask of yourself; on the reverse side was a list of the rewards that might be considered for associates.

At a minimum, Al reviewed these cards monthly to remind himself of his obligation to his associates. His function was to be sure every staff member was encouraged to learn more about the job; on-going training, if you will.

In the Pharmacy Nursing Home division, monitoring for accuracy was absolutely essential. Each patient was assigned a drawer with dividers for various times of the day. The technician placed the drug in the proper drawer, the pharmacist checked each drawer, and the administering nurse had the same information and checked once again.

In addition to the first pharmacist, another pharmacist checked at regular intervals for any possible mistakes. In effect, the medication was monitored four different times. This system of dispensing saved the nursing homes hundreds of man-hours in administering medicine.

Whenever there are good ideas introduced, some imaginative soul finds a way to improve on it- and improve they did. One young man on Al's staff recommended that each medication be enclosed in a sealed cellophane package identified by both the medication's name and its strength. This resulted in a decided improvement in both safety and sanitation. Customer's appreciated the modification and the improved efficiencies within Al's operation were evident as well. In addition, several new customers were added because of this innovation.

The young man who promoted the concept internally was offered an opportunity to buy into the company and was put in charge of the nursing home division with the economic rewards to go with it.

Ode to Mr. Grube

This story starts in '55
The dream of just one man
To start a little business
Al Grube had a plan.

The Grube sign went up that year
With Grant's and Carl's Shoes
Woolworth's and a grocery store
Three Sisters, Hi-Lo Bakery too.

He struggled through some lean years
Though there never was a doubt
This man would get himself a team
And lead us in the shout.

He is skilled at being a thespian
That is thespian, T. H.
He donned a skirt and sweater once
His cheerleading was really great.

He is always fair and friendly
And he knows us all by name
He makes us all feel special
And treats us all the same.

The store has changed and grown some
Throughout these forty years
And Al was there through thick and thin
He deserves at least three cheers!

So on this day we honor you
With love and admiration
And let us be the first to say
Our heartfelt CONGRATULATIONS!

written by Cheryl Lopour, May, 1995.

8. Measure

To Measure is to evaluate the levels of achievement.

Are we accomplishing our goals? Are we doing better or worse? What should or could be changed?

The ultimate goal is profit, the return for investment of capital and time. Since there are many factors affecting profit, there must be some way to intelligently measure these factors and control them within reasonable bounds. Just one area grossly out of balance can reduce or even obliterate profit.

Correcting factors that have gone awry, and the energy and effort needed to regain balance, can be costly in both time and dollars. Effective measurement can reveal problems before they get out of hand.

There are at least eight focal points in most businesses:
1) Customers
2) Associates
3) Owners
4) The community
5) Managing Capital
6) Marketing
7) Taxes
8) Cash flow

The eight factors vary in importance for each kind of business. Some factors are more easily controlled than others. Typically, the area that has the biggest impact on the bottom line receives the most attention.

Al's comments reflect his views as a retailer. Ken, who was involved in manufacturing for most of his career, has a different set of priorities.

Ken measures progress

Ken believes that each business must find ways to specifically measure its goals and mission to be effective and profitable. The business must find relevant measurements of its net profit, inventory turn, return on assets, labor costs, and before and after tax consequences.

Measurement should be designed to fill a specific purpose before it is undertaken. If you don't know what you are measuring or why you are measuring, don't measure—your measurements will be totally meaningless. Look to other successful businesses in creating a model for measurement. Establish meaningful measurements within your business based on the success of others.

If you have a clear mission statement of what your business is all about, your first measurement should encompass the global mission of your enterprise. Measuring the big picture will help you honestly determine whether or not you are truly accomplishing your mission and will serve as a screen eliminating distracting work. This big first measurement will help unearth many deficiencies you might otherwise miss; it will help keep you on track.

As you work your way down through your organization, the measurement of goals will become more and more specific. There are many sophisticated accounting tools that will be helpful in managing your business. The two key questions to ask are: 1) Are the measurements germane to my enterprise? and 2) Are the measurements timely?

Reams of accounting and statistical data often are not relevant to the measurement of your business. On the other hand, if the data is relevant but available only long after the decision point, it won't be of any help to you.

This short book is not an accounting text or tutorial on statistical analysis. It is far more basic than that. Here we are asking the simple, general and dumb questions that are often overlooked in our zeal to process data that may give the appearance of sophisticated analysis.

Some years ago there was a salad oil scandal that shook the confidence of bankers and businessmen alike. The bankers and the lawyers had carefully drafted and honed piles of finely printed documents identifying the gigantic tanks of salad oil, precisely stating the loan covenants necessary to secure the loans as well as specific measurements for compliance. The experts had done their work well except for one basic measurement: Were the huge salad oil tanks full of salad oil? The answer was no. The tanks were all full of water with only a thin layer of salad oil floating on top of the water. Unfortunately, the money had been loaned before anyone ever thought of the first basic measure: full tanks of salad oil.

The auto industry is faced with similar questions. Is the SUV the vehicle for the future? The first measurement might be the cost of a full tank of gas and how its consumption affects the environment.

We must always remember our owners, customers, communities, and associates in this process of measurement. This universe must be balanced if the business is to succeed.

Al measured key factors

Al concentrated on monitoring those factors that had the biggest impact on his sales and profit They included the customer, inventory control, advertising and other factors like good will.

The number of customers impacts immediately on the bottom line in retail. With many customers, you can afford to make some mistakes; with few, there is little cash flow and no future. A simple measurement tool for this is the customer count. How many folks came in and made a purchase? This measures the effectiveness of the advertising and other promotions.

Purchase per customer is a measure of the effectiveness of your associates. It also measures the effectiveness of advertising as well as merchandising when well-displayed product turns over.

It is also important to measure shrinkage due to customer theft. This can be a disaster for a retail business and is attributable to a number of different scenarios, such as an insufficient number of associates, associates who are not observant, and products that are hidden from the associates' view. The goal at Grube Pharmacy was to serve the customer well, discourage theft, and increase the amount each customer purchased.

Inventory should reflect what the customer expects to find in a particular type of store. Marginal items or different products can be carried, but the basic inventory should not create a series of surprises. It should be what the customer expects to find.

Product turnover is important. High turnover offers quantity buying discounts from suppliers. Turnover can be easily monitored with computers, adding when stock comes in, subtracting when a sale occurs. In retail, the higher the turnover, the lower the investment and the greater the probability of being profitable. It is relatively easy to create a disciplined reorder plan, because most computers have that capability right from the start.

Product sales vary dramatically and different seasons impact sales activity. In addition, sales vary as customer appeal changes. Today's hot item is tomorrow's dog. Like some other things in life, 20 per cent of the items represent 80 per cent of the sales. Yet the 80 per cent of stock that sells slowly contribute to what consumers perceive as a well-stocked store worthy of a visit. Competing mini-marts carry only the fast sellers. There is always a part of the 80 per cent that has become obsolete and should be phased out. These challenges are what make retailing a game as well as a business.

Every organization needs equipment to get things done. It is a huge investment. All pieces require regular maintenance. Sometimes we put this off only to suffer a breakdown. We then incur costs to return the equipment to full production and extra costs in time lost.

Merchandising is critical to retail. It is about the placement and organization of product to attract the consumers attention and to encourage a purchase. Good signage makes merchandising more effective. While signage is an important ingredient to sales success, it cannot be measured very easily.

Measuring advertising

Advertising can be effective, but it is also problematic because accurate, direct measurement of its impact is difficult. Advertising is commonly measured by impression numbers, the circulation of a newspaper or number of listeners of a radio station. This method is never conclusive as there is no way to tell how many readers or listeners paid attention to the ad and acted on it.

Therefore, cost-benefit analysis of media advertising is difficult to evaluate. The up-front charge is known from the beginning, but there is no simple way to prove it has been effective. What did you get for your expenditure? The questions cannot be answered except by guesswork.

The mantra of all sellers of advertising is that continuity is essential in order for the advertising campaign to be successful. But there is no direct way to measure something definitive like "we added 40 new customers" or "our sales increased by 15 per cent because of an ad that we ran." Advertising is essential to the success of any business, but measurement of direct results is often cloaked in ambiguity because of the many other factors in addition to advertising that are required for success.

Retailers are constantly looking for ways to increase store traffic. Considering all the advertising and the sales all the retailers run, it is obvious they want to motivate potential customers to come into their stores.

Although Al advertised and ran sales events, his most successful approach was to have a service counter centered around a post office. This service counter rendered many other services, from passport photos to selling tickets for local fund-raisers and entertainment productions, but the post office was by far the most effective draw.

One of Al's cashiers expressed an interest in being responsible for the post office, so she was put in charge. Her efforts quickly raised the annual volume of the post office to more than $1 million a year in a time when postage was less than half today's rates. During her tenure, the store was never short more than $5 for any year.

Hundreds of people came in daily to use those services. While the store could not make a profit from postal services, the U. S. Postal Service paid Grube's $4000 a year for providing this service to the community.

Almost seven years after he retired, a personal visit to the local main post office brought the following comment from one of the postal clerks, "aren't you Al Grube from the drugstore? We sure miss your post office. Our work load has really increased since that post office closed."

It is true that not everyone who used the postal service bought something from the drugstore with every visit, but many did. More importantly, Grube's became their store for drugs, especially prescriptions, the main reason for its existence.

Since Grube Pharmacy was about 25 years younger than any of its 18 competitors, it was quite exciting when Grube's sales volume left the others behind. Measuring goals can also be fun.

9. Fair Compensation

Fair Compensation is the relationship between the earnings of your associates and others.

Fair compensation is in the eye of the beholder. It is obvious that to remain competitive with other businesses in your industry, you must pay competitive wages or you will find yourself in a continuous search for employees.

You will not necessarily be forced to match the highest bidder. On the contrary, if you establish a fair and understandable plan that is candidly shared with your associates and fully understood and honestly executed, you will very quickly be the employment place of preference.

We would suggest that the more opportunities you create for additional compensation based on company profitability, the more involvement your associates will display. Your objective is to create a climate that is fair in the eyes of your associates and fair in practice as well. It must be shared with everyone and applied consistently. Not everyone will agree with the range levels, but consistency will eliminate or greatly reduce challenges to the system.

Motivating associates

Associates are essential to meet the needs of the consumer and to perform the myriad of activities needed to sustain any business. Usually the need for help is greater than the price one can afford to pay, which suggests priorities must be established.

Salary or compensation becomes a conundrum. Most employers can afford to pay approximately the going rate for a person's service based on what is paid by the market for the same type of service. If you pay too much you will not make a profit. If you pay too little, you spend all your time hiring and training new help and profit will also suffer.

As with most things, you get what you pay for. It is worth it to offer a competitive starting wage and include opportunities for the associate to increase his or her income. Offer increases based on a longevity as well as rewards for sales successes. This system seems to work better than a static one; as the associate becomes worth more, they are paid more. This approach has decided merit.

Bonuses should be based on the premise that if the company can make more money, it can afford to pay more money to associates. Al believed in that idea. He has always favored a two-tiered system, basic pay plus some form of profit-sharing.

He used what he called "PM" (for Profit Merchandise), a sales bonus for selling more expensive items. It was to be paid at least once a month, the closer to the sale, the better. The compensation was paid by separate check. This made it more meaningful and impressed upon the worker that it was something extra for doing more.

Fringe benefits are always nice and a very important perk, but at times costly. Health insurance is a classic example. It is a very desirable perk, which everyone should have, but many organizations cannot absorb such high costs. This may be why many other countries have universal health care.

When everyone shares in successes, it is great for both teamwork and interest in the outcome. Fair compensation has to include everyone involved in a project, not just a select few.

A System for Fair Compensation

What follows is an example which demonstrates the approach we recommend. The dollar amounts are examples, and will vary depending on the business.

A base salary is set first. It is for the lowest-paid associate whose services have a minimal impact on the company's profitability. Let us select $10 per hour for the lowest-paid associate, who, like the majority of his or her counterparts, works 40 hours per week.

All associates should receive a multiple of that base salary. Here are the multiples for computing levels of base compensation before computing any bonus pay:

1. New hires for basic labor receive the base salary of $10 per hour or $400 per week.

2. The immediate superior to those receiving the base salary would receive two times the base or $20 per hour ($800 per week).

3. Low middle managers would receive three times the base or $30 per hour ($1,200 per week).

4. High middle managers and those with specialty training would receive four times base or $40 per hour ($1,600 per week).

5. Top executives would receive six times the base or $60 per hour ($2,400 per week).

6. The president and CEO would receive 15 times the base or $150 per hour ($6,000 per week).

Longevity raises would be consistent throughout. For each additional year of employment, each employee would receive 25 cents per hour in addition to their base hourly wage. The additional reward recognizes that longevity increases knowledge. This is recognized without overtaxing the wage structure. However, longevity compensation should not be an incentive for just hanging on without significant contribution to the business.

Health Care Benefits: The company absorbs 75 per cent of the associates health care cost, but the employee is responsible for 25 per cent: as health care costs increase, the associates' outlay is also increased. Health care costs are split 50–50 for members of the associate's family, with the associate paying half and the employer paying half. Since almost 60 per cent of spouses are employed elsewhere, their mates could also receive benefits from their employer. This provides an incentive to share the burden.

Pensions could be paid by setting aside 5 per cent of pre-tax profits for payment into a retirement fund for each associate. The amount paid into each retirement fund would be based on the salary each receives. An outside investment firm should be charged with managing the retirement pension funds, which could be invested in securities.

Profit-sharing bonuses should be paid from a pool of money created by setting aside 20 per cent of pre-tax profits. These bonuses would also vary by salary level and would only be paid when the business makes a profit.

The option for an associate to use profit-sharing dollars in whatever way he or she chooses is important. The company plan should also provide for ownership, allowing associates to purchase company stock at a discount. This would serve a number of useful purposes: increased interest in company profitability, longevity, and loyalty.

Capital investment is also important. A fair percentage of the after-tax profits should be allocated to capital and the balance of the after-tax profit could be used to pay dividends to shareholders. For example, 70 per cent of the after-tax profit could be used for capital and 30 per cent for dividends.

With a system like the one just outlined, all participants have an incentive to increase profitability. Company financial reports should be available for all associates and stockholders, permitting all participants to be equally informed.

Other areas that might prove useful would be to require that 25 per cent of the board of directors be union members or representatives of the associates. There could be incentives for other activities such as quitting smoking, having good attendance, starting an exercise program, and participating in community projects.

A plan will not work unless it makes good sense, and is promoted candidly and extensively throughout the organization. Quarterly reports revealing the details of the business operations should produce the desired results. The entire organization should have a spirit of cost consciousness, interest in profitability, and a strong team spirit.

Fair compensation will only be believed by your staff if they are informed of the policy you are using. This information must be shared consistently, with reminders on at least an annual basis. The associates may not agree with your policy, but they will understand it and trust you more for it. Fair compensation will be understood and acknowledged by all associates if they can see it, read it, and talk about it, knowing that everyone is receiving the same accurate information. Knowledge is very, powerful. When the associate is told up-front, the plan is always more readily acceptable. The unknown breeds dissatisfaction, speculation and discontent.

In a typical business today, only the board of directors and the top level employees know how additional compensation is rewarded. Rewards unrelated to productivity or profitability are an absolute waste of money and accomplish nothing except to make the recipients wealthier. They verify the gullibility of the people responsible for hiring these overpaid executives.

We recommend making incomes of all associates known and available to all. This encourages competitiveness, respect for the leaders and the stimuli to get potential leaders to try to improve.

In smaller businesses, fewer compensation levels make sense. For example, Al's card and gift store had only three levels; sales clerks, middle management, and the store manager. Annual longevity raises distinguished seasoned associates from new hires. A bonus for higher sales could increase one's income by as much as 40 per cent. Since the sales bonus was paid on a separate check each month, it was a reminder twelve times a year that extra effort pays off.

The drugstore was a larger business with special requirements. It was mandatory that the pharmacists received higher compensation for their investment in education. Al added assignments to their middle management responsibilities, and bonuses for profitability.

The level of top executive compensation in many businesses today is unconscionable. Executives earning more than 800 times the average compensation of everyone else in the business is unmitigated greed. If an executive earns fifteen times that of the working folks, with the remainder of his or her earnings tied to an equitable bonus system that also fairly recognizes the work of everyone else in the business, the business will prosper without ill will.

No one should ever receive a bonus from an entity that is losing money. To pay an executive a bonus when the company is losing money only incites those who are asked to buckle down or take a pay cut.

It is important to separate returns to capital from wages and salaries paid to workers when discussing this issue. Often the public misunderstands the difference, lumping them both together and crying, "rip off!" A fair return on money invested should not be combined and identified as part of the salary of an executive. The returns from investment should remain separate from salary, which is an expense for the business. However, when a company plays fast and loose with stock options, the total an executive receives must be placed under the spotlight for careful scrutiny.

Should more government control greedy business executives of big public corporations? Perhaps, but keep in mind that the problem is also an ethical one that may easily occur in both large private and small businesses as well. It is easy to seek regulation of everyone except the accuser. It is more difficult to candidly examine the problem when we may be part of it.

The majority of businesses executives probably resent being swept into the dark hole of "greed". Yet, there is a sort of "good old boy" network among compensation committees that determines "fair compensation" knowing that what the committee determines for others will also be what they themselves receive. It's an ethical trap; high pay generates high pay for me. When my peers study my compensation, they will do for me, what I have done for them. It's time that every board of directors study the way they determine executive compensation.

Businessmen and women must themselves evaluate what they have done to erode the system by injecting cynicism rather than trust, and greed rather than fairness. Greed will always be with us, but to let it run rampant will lead to an autocratic government and fewer well-to-do people than we presently have.

Fair compensation should include everyone involved in a business, not just a select few.

10. Profit

Profit is the money remaining after all expenses have been satisfied.

Profit is the goal of every business. The more profit a business makes, the more successful it is judged to be. The underlying narrative of the first nine chapters of Book Two is about how a business can make a large and sustainable profit.

The quest for profit is good for both the business involved and the society it serves. When we seek profits, we are motivated to take risks with our time and our capital. Profit is a reward for taking that risk. While not the only reward—profit also creates emotional rewards—it is the one that society recognizes and applauds us for when we succeed.

The drive for profit affects more than just the enterprise; it is also a primary motivator for societal advancement. It drives discoveries that will improve our lives, increase life expectancy, increase productivity, and in general, enhance our standard of living. Of course, the pursuit of profit can have a downside, but the basic trajectory for society is for the better.

How to make a profit gets the lion's share of attention in this and most business books. What is not discussed as much is what happens next. What is done with the profit after it is generated? Those who accumulate profit must understand that obligations are created to distribute the profit in a judicious, fair and meaningful manner. A fair distribution of profit is important for all involved, the workers, the community, and for ability of the business itself to produce profit in the future.

This final chapter will discuss this second part of the profit equation.

Profit means four things for the business and for the community it serves. It provides Rewards, permits Growth, allows for Enhancements to the business and how it operates, and can be used to benefit the Community.

As we have said previously, some of the profit should be shared with those who help generate it. It should be used for **Rewards** for these people. Our suggestion is to share 20 per cent of pre-tax net profit with employees. Once taxes are paid, about 30 per cent should be paid to investors in the form of dividends, while the remaining 70 per cent used for investment in growth. We believe that with appropriate incentives, people become motivated and the enterprise become successful.

Growth is only possible in the long-run if profit is earned by a business.

Growth is the insatiable consumer of funds; it increases the need for more facilities, inventory, equipment, and people. All are inter-related; investing in one area automatically creates needs in the other three areas. The plan for growth requires thought and intelligent planning. When growth is out of control or is irrational and unfocused, it becomes a weed that strangles the business.

The creation of profit requires the judicious use of capital. Profit, like life, is about the attention to detail and about intelligent long-range planning. By themselves, these details seem to affect only small amounts of money, but cumulatively, they add up to large sums.

Enhancements represent the ego side of the division of profit. It is the upgrading of everything from physical facilities and equipment to the perks provided for the staff. Enhancements are things that are not really essential, but are like the desert that finishes a delicious meal. Enhancements send a message to the community that you are a special place. In the long-run, you will attract better employees, will be more welcome in the community, and you will become the preferred choice of consumers.

Community involvement usually receives the smallest share of profits. However, it often has the longest-enduring effect on the image of your company. Whether you have one facility or multiple ones in diverse regions, your contributions to your community will be recognized, remembered, and your people revered.

Community involvement can be either physical efforts on the part of the company's associates or it can be a financial contribution from the company to worthy community causes, or a combination of both.

Al has always believed that sharing profits is a key way to motivate associates. He used two approaches for the distribution of the profits from his business. In the pharmacy, the four principals, each responsible for a division and each owning stock, could watch the value of their stock increase as the company became more profitable. In addition, the company invested five per cent of each employee's earnings in a growth mutual fund that was reserved for them and its value was reported annually.

For the card and gift division, the company invested five per cent of each employee's earnings in an accumulation fund if the store was profitable. It acted as a savings account and each employee received an annual report from the accountants. In addition, each received a monthly check, separate from payroll, that equaled five per cent of the sales each employee made of items that cost more than $35 each. December sales generated the most additional compensation.

The amount paid to each employee is not as significant as simply the chance to earn extra money. The extra pay becomes a sense of pride. For some, it meant "mad money" to be spent frivolously. Believe me, that seemed to be a very important motivating factor.

Although "sharing profit" is used by only a minority of small businesses, its positive effect on those businesses is appreciable. To ignore that useful tool is penny-wise and pound-foolish.

Personnel are an integral part of most businesses. When they give one hundred per cent, it is because there is something in it for them. Try as you will, without sharing the profit, you do not get the maximum return. Growth is stymied or retarded. People must be involved.

Epilogue

Thank you for reading *Pathways to Success*. The mission of this book is to encourage the leaders of today to consider their associates as the most important part of their team. Not only are they the actual producers of the products and services, but their knowledge and experience can lead to dynamic improvements in those products and services.

Each chapter reinforces our belief that the key to our success was that we capitalized on our most valuable assets, our associates.

Bear in mind that in the majority of organizations, your most valuable assets are also your largest operational cost. Prudence requires you to maximize your returns on this large expenditure.

A clear and concise VISION establishes direction, which enhances the ability to conceptualize what you wish to achieve for your business.

If your vision is consistent with the MISSION statement developed by you and your colleagues, you will be on the pathway to success.

All your communication must be done with CANDOR, or you will be suspect of different treatment for different associates. Consistency is absolutely essential and always being up-front with your associates will demonstrate your fairness and your sincerity. You will garner respect for being truthful and straight-forward.

TRUST is the ultimate goal; when trust is established, your organization will run smoothly. Everyone will be looking out for each other and productivity will improve. Costs will be minimized and the quality of product and service will be maximized. There is no better way to increase profit and reduce turnover. The general response from associates will be, "I like it here!"

It is this positive environment in which SPIRIT will prevail. People will share and support one another, because spirit puts the frosting on the cake. When people have fun, and enjoy what they are doing, their productivity increases many-fold. People who enjoy what they are doing do not want to leave and work elsewhere. With longevity comes experience, understanding, and increased productivity.

Your efforts cannot help but strengthen the COMMITMENT. Committed people get more done, in less time, and more effectively. A better product or service is the obvious result. This, in turn, makes the company more attractive to do business with and creates an attraction for the superior associates to join your company. The winners always attract a higher caliber of available associates.

Progress and problems must be MONITORED to be sure the direction you desire is functioning as planned. It is the logical way to discover problems so that measures can be taken to correct them.

In most instances the early discovery can be more easily corrected and the cost of potential losses can be mitigated. "Lose a little, not a lot," is a good mantra.

Comparison is a great tool to determine how you are doing. To compare you must MEASURE your goals to determine if you are improving or losing ground. Obviously, if you're improving you want to do more of the same, but if you are losing ground, change must be considered and quickly implemented. The three key questions really are: measure when change is possible, measure when the information is current and usable, and measure when you are in a position to change. Those three rules are effective if you are considering whether to measure or not to measure. Improvement is everyone's goal.

Although FAIR COMPENSATION is in the eye of the beholder, the standards are usually set in an established industry, so it is difficult to deviate too dramatically. Here innovation can spell the difference in attracting people of desired skills. Productivity and profitability can be rewarded, setting your compensation apart from others in your market. It is really the "share" philosophy; the more you produce, the larger your reward.

The key to this concept is to make the information available to all. It must be shared, discussed, reminded of, and an issue must be made of successes. If the rewards are available to all, without prejudice, it is fair.

PROFIT is the reason for risk, for productivity, for investment, and for effort. If the rewards are shared in a fair way, profit will increase and continue to increase as long as integrity is the backbone of the philosophy being followed.

Success can be yours if you practice these ten guidelines diligently. Your rewards will be gratifying far beyond the compensation you accrue. Your job will be fun, your relationships meaningful, and your accolades will be many.

Only you can determine the level of success you will reach.

Appendix

We include two examples of how Al handled personnel issues. The first example is how associates were carefully instructed about how to deal with customers. Two "15 Points" lists were printed on cards, laminated and given to each associate at Mary Lee's Hallmark store. They were to be carried in uniform pockets as reminders that "We are a Model of Good Cusotmer Service."

15 Points to Good Floor Service

1. Be aware of Customer's presence -
2. Make customer feel welcome -
3. Accept customer as they are and give them your full attention -
4. Establish trust -
5. Be friendly, enthusiastic and sincere -
6. Discover customers needs with questions -
7. Problem solve to meet needs -
8. Match their needs with benefits of product -
9. Present and handle merchandise professionally -
10. Involve customer with merchandise -
11. Find substitute if necessary -
12. Suggest add-on item -
13. Ask for sale -
14. Assist or direct customer to the register -
15. Thank the customer -

15 Points to Good Register Service

1. Stand up straight, look alert, friendly and interested -
2. Smile and make eye contact -
3. Start with a friendly greeting -
4. Use name recognition if possible -
5. Ask for Gold Crown card -
6. Ring each item, call attention to sale items -
7. Compliment or comment on an item -
8. Suggest potential add-on sale -
9. Announce total -
10. Repeat total and amount of tender -
11. Place bill on tray -
12. Count change into customers hand -
13. Place bill in drawer -
14. Give customer receipt with sincere "Thank You" -
15. Invite customer back with upcoming event or offer -

To the customer the sales associates ARE the business. The "15 Points to Good Floor Service" are necessary and important to perform in order to be reasonably certain the customers were always given the best service possible. The "15 Points to Good Register Service" guaranteed consistent performance and behavior by sales associates when assisting customers at the cash register. We believed that customers had the right to be treated in a consistent manner in all aspects of the business.

Beginning on page 184 is the four-page version of the employee manual issued by Mary Lee's Hallmark. This mini-manual covers the issues that employees most frequently ask about. A detailed personel manual was also available for each associate to consult whenever they wished.

The mini-manual is divided into four sections:

1. Welcome, a bit of rah-rahs, and a few expectations.
2. Purpose of policies.
3. Basic benefits and how these benefits are applied to their position.
4. A discussion of 16 areas responsible for most of the problems.

This brief manual is easy for the associate to digest. Assoicates should be able to integrate into the system with a minimum of confusion on their part. Reviewing this booklet with the new associate and presenting them with a copy saved time and avoided misunderstandings.

The chart on page 2 of the booklet shows when various perks would be available to the new associate. The chart shows the number of hours an associate had to work to qualify for each of the benefits. By doing it in steps, the associates enjoyed the little rewards at intervals and were eager to visit with their supervisor because there was something in it for them.

Different amounts of time on the job were required to move up to the next level, along with passing a simple test. Time was set aside for discussion between associate and superviser as each new step was attained. When people visit with one another they have an opportunity to begin to develop a relationship. It is an ideal time to begin the creation of trust.

Trust on the employees part is greatly enhanced when they know that the rules are applied consistently to all of the associates; most important, of course, to them is themselves.

Al thought it essential to also have a detailed personnel manual that spelled out a broad range of rules that covered the most common situations, along with guidelines on how to use and apply the rules.

Personnel manuals are essential to a company's successful functioning, but their value lies in keeping them current and consistent. The manual must be available to all associates.

Welcome to Mary Lee's Hallmark!

We are confident that you will do all in your power to guarantee the highest level of customer satisfaction, for, to our customers, you are Mary Lee's whenever you serve them.

Our vision statement says "**We are a model of quality and service treating our customers and associates as friends**". Please accept our vision as your credo as well.

Historically speaking, Mary Lee's was purchased from Hallmark, Inc. in 1984, by the principals in Grube Pharmacies, Inc.. Grube's provided administrative services and operational support. We sold the pharmacy divisions, both Pharmacare and Pharmacy, and Mary Lee's became Grube Pharmacies, Inc. only operating division.

This brief summary will give you a glimpse of what's in it for you and some of our expectations.

Communication is the foundation of a satisfying relationship. No question is too dumb or inappropriate. We will do our best to answer any of your questions.

Our benefit schedule is designed to be fair and reasonable for all concerned. That includes you, your fellow associates and the company.

A full-time associate must work 30 hours per week or more. All the steps that are listed below require a minimum of 30 days between levels and a minimum number of hours.

1

Mary Lee's
Hallmark
GOLD CROWN ®

<u>Purpose of our policy</u>

A.   To demonstrate that WE CARE about our associates.

B.   To demonstrate that we accept input from our associates.

C.   To assure Mary Lee's associates that we are competitive in payroll in this market place.

D.   To reduce associate turnover.

E.   To encourage promotion from within to positions of increased responsibility.

<u>Benefit Schedules</u>

STATUS	HOURS MIN	MONTHS MIN	RATE	TEST	NOTES
Hire				Math	
Store Charge	64.5	1		*	Credit Limit Applies
Discounts	130	2	20%	*	Personal Purchases
Probation	390	3	$0.35	*	Raise Eligible
401K	750	3*	0	*	Investment
PM's	780	6	5%	*	Preselected Product
Raise	1070	9	$0.50	*	Managers Satisfied
STA Begins to Count	1500	12*	Earned Income to Total Incomes	*	Profit Sharing
Longevity	1500	12	BOD		BOD Decides Amount
Time & 1/2 Sundays/Holidays	Top of Scale	12	Team Leader Eligible		

Customer benefits, such as the use of a Gold Crown Card are available to you at once--if you desire.

2

Mary Lee's
Hallmark

<u>Vacation</u>   Full Time:
                    After: One year   One Week
                             Two years   Two Weeks
                             Ten years   Three Weeks
                             Twenty five years   Four Weeks

                                        Part Time:
                    After: Five years   One Week
                             Ten years   Two Weeks

<u>Health Insurance</u> is available for full time associates: the associate
pays 100% of the premium for the first three months, 50% of the
premium for the next nine months, and Mary Lee's pays it all after that
<u>base</u> year, after which the associate only pays 50% of the increase of
the cost of the premiums.

<u>Smocks</u>--2 for part time or 3 for full time, and we monitor for
replacement annually.

Our expectations from you are:

1)   All associates are expected to work some nights, weekends, and
        holidays. This is subject to change as necessity requires.
2)   The associates are responsible for their assigned schedule
        coverage with fellow associates with similar skills--this includes
        illness, personal events, and family concerns. We will schedule
        replacements for preplanned vacations longer than three days.
3)   Punctuality is expected--so that others do not have to alter
        their plans for your convenience.
4)   Monthly meeting attendance is mandatory. Meetings are usually
        on the first Monday evening of the month from 9:15 - 10:30
        pm. Acceptable excuses are vacation, hospitalization, and
        death.
5)   Breaks are 10 minutes in length. We prefer that you are
        available (in the store) for personal phone calls, bathroom stops,
        smoking (outside), and snacking are done on breaks. If you
        work a six hour shift you get a 30 minute lunch break.
6)   Lunch is 30 minutes unless other arrangements are made. You
        may leave the store, but please return on time so no one else is
        inconvenienced.
7)   No soda, food, or any edibles are permitted in the front of the
        store.

3

8)   Associate credit limit is based on one week's gross salary for the first continuous six months of employment after which you may charge what you can pay for in the next 30 days.

9)   20% discounts are honored for all associates purchases (see policy in the benefit schedule listed previously) provided the products are for your personal use, or that of a family member who is dependent on you for a portion of their livelihood and resides in your home.

10)   Dishonesty and theft are part of your responsibility to report if observed.

11)   PM's (when you become eligible) are paid for your participation in the sale. It is unfair to take credit for a customer's carry up or another associate's efforts.

12)   Purchasing of limited editions (no discounts allowed) or limited quantities are controlled by the manager. We will share, but at least half of the product must be available for our customers.

13)   Consumption of salable edibles is at the sole discretion of the manager. In other words, do not eat the candy!

14)   All products given to the store are store property for disposal at the owners' discretion.

15)   Teamwork and knowledge sharing is expected from all associates.

16)   Everyone is expected to share in the chores. Your hourly rate is paid to compensate for that effort. PM's are a plus for your sales skills.

Learning and advancing are part of your responsibility. Please do not hesitate to ask. Each of your colleagues are dedicated to helping you learn and earn.

We are willing to share--it's up to you to help us make money so there is something to share.

We hope you enjoy being an important part of Mary Lee's Hallmark.

Mary & Al
Grube

4

www.ingramcontent.com/pod-product-compliance
Lightning Source LLC
Chambersburg PA
CBHW071427170526
45165CB00001B/421